The Asset Mindset

The Asset Mindset

A Special Forces Perspective for Achieving Success

Daniel Fielding

TheAssetMindset.com

Published by Tablo

Table of Contents

Reviews

The Asset Mindset gives **PEOPLE AN ADVANTAGE by allowing us to PERSEVERE BEYOND THE OBSTACLES we face.** As a retired Chief Warrant Officer of the Marine Corps, I never thought I would benefit from reading a book meant to change my perspective on life. More importantly, I realized I would have had an easier time during my challenging life moments had I approached things with the tools in "The Asset Mindset." This book does not require anyone to change their life, but rather look at life with a new perspective on challenges and opportunities. Decision making in life is where people succeed or fail. Everybody at some point in their life applies most of these tools Dan spells out, but having a solid roadmap to plan and approach things in a methodical way will help anyone. I feel I will benefit from applying his approach to life's decisions, and I plan to instill his approaches as I raise my young boys to be strong men. I hope this book gets in the hands of teenagers as they step into the world and need to make choices of their own, as well as be picked up by adults in mid-stride of their current life's journey. This book is a great read for anyone no matter where they find themselves. I gained a new perspective on life's challenges and opportunities, and I believe it will do the same for others.

Christopher Nochera
Chief Warrant Officer, U.S. Marine Corps, (Ret)

What does it take to be an asset and think like an elite Special Forces operator? In *The Asset Mindset*, Dan Fielding invites readers on an intimate journey—from behind the scenes on Special Forces deployments to backstage with Kid Rock—and shares the impactful life lessons that set the stage for success in a multitude of circumstances. Along the way, he introduces readers to a cast of unforgettable individuals—from Fielding's own family, to Special Forces soldiers and the most unlikely Green Beret candidate called "Littleman" who eventually became a Delta operator—and the gifts of wisdom that they each contributed to his own Asset Mindset. I've worked as a writer with Special Operations personnel for years, and what is unique about Dan's approach is that he offers advice that is accessible to anyone. It is impossible to read this book and not walk away with your life enriched; in his signature warm, engaging, and wise tone, Fielding invites readers to walk with him on a path of self-development that is rarely easy, but always worthwhile. The Asset Mindset is a critical tool for anyone facing adversity or looking for insight into the mental aspect of personal development that will give them an edge to be successful in any scenario. By the time you're done reading, you'll feel like Dan is a close personal friend, and you'll be eager to get started putting *The Asset Mindset* to use!

Dr. Alice Atalanta, Ph.D.
Author, Collaborator, and Veteran's Advocate

This book is a GREAT RESOURCE for anyone looking to improve their life! I thoroughly enjoyed Daniel Fielding's book *The Asset Mindset*. As a former Green Beret myself, I really appreciate how Dan has so clearly and entertainingly explained how to apply the lessons we learned in the U.S. Army Special Forces so that anyone can learn how to live a more productive and rewarding life.

Kurt Webber
LTC, U.S. Army (Ret)
Founder and President of Camp Resilience Program for Veterans

The Asset Mindset **is INSPIRING and REJUVENATING!** Daniel Fielding, a former Green Beret soldier explains, in great detail, how to apply the essential life altering traits he acquired as a Special Forces Operator to your everyday life. Daniel offers more than just advice. He teaches a winning lifestyle that, when utilized, can only lead to a more rewarding, successful, and satisfying life. I recommend reading *The Asset Mindset* again and again, whenever you need a boost and motivation to get back on track toward achieving your goals and dreams. No matter what stage of life or career you are in, you will benefit greatly from the insights revealed by Daniel Fielding, just as I did.

Thomas M. Cirignano
Author of "The Constant Outsider: Memoirs of a South Boston Mechanic" and "67 Cents: Creation of a South Boston Killer".

Foreword

When I received the draft of this manuscript, I was surprised by the content. I had anticipated it was going to be completely about Daniel Fielding's experiences while conducting the many harrowing and extremely dangerous missions he had been on as a Special Forces soldier. I knew he had been sent on numerous operations in other faraway, hostile lands. I was aware that several of his close "brothers" and comrades had not been fortunate enough to return home from those missions alive. I thought that maybe he wanted to tell those stories of heroism, but that was not the case. I hope he writes a sequel some day, as I really want to hear more about those missions; that is, if special-ops soldiers are even allowed to share those details.

While Daniel does touch upon some details of missions, his book is more about explaining the intense training which helped him to be successful in Special Forces, and the mindset which played a big part in his ability to return home in one piece. Daniel's intent is plain and simple, which he conveys in clear, simple language that can touch any reader. He strives to give his readers the same valuable tools that kept him alive while on Special Forces missions; tools which still serve him well to this day. He talks at length about the attributes which his Special Forces training had imprinted into his psyche. He refers to utilizing the sum of those tools as having *The Asset Mindset*. These mindset-skills are still allowing him to achieve great things in his post military, civilian life, as you will read.

I must make a full disclosure. I am no stranger to the author of this book. I have known Daniel Fielding's parents for over 50 years. It has been one of the true blessings in my life having them as cherished and close friends.

It's no surprise to me that Daniel turned out to be the courageous and inspiring person that he is. Parental influence had lots to do with it. As they say, "The apple doesn't fall far from the tree." I still remember the day I went over to their home to see Guy and Mary Ellen's days old baby boy many years ago. I never imagined that the baby I was holding would someday become a Special Forces Green Beret warrior. It gives me chills thinking about it! It takes a very special kind of person to put his or her own life on the line in service to their fellow man and country. Daniel is that special kind of person, and I'm proud to call him my friend.

Knowing that I had published two books several years ago, Daniel asked if I would consider looking at a book he was writing. Of course, I said I would be happy to. After all, that is the way friends should treat each other. His family has always been there for me, and I try to do the same.

Finding and maintaining a positive attitude in today's increasingly negative environment is not an easy task. Just watch the evening news to see examples. But, Daniel's *Asset Mindset* will change the way we deal with the negativity and obstacles we encounter. We will all face negativity throughout our lives, and inspiration is an increasingly rare commodity. This book is inspiring. But please don't think you can read *The Asset Mindset* just once and it will change your life. It takes time and effort to create new habits and change the way we think. I've already read this book twice, and I got more out of it the second time. Reading it again reinforced the important points I read the first time and helped remind me how to bring more positivity into every day of my life. I know it will do the same for you. This is a book that should not be put away in a bookcase. I hope you will keep it in a prominent spot, where it is visible. Pick it up and read it again whenever you need inspiration, and share it with those you love.

Thomas M. Cirignano
Author of "The Constant Outsider: Memoirs of a South Boston
Mechanic" and "67 Cents: Creation of a South Boston Killer".

Introduction

"You can't come off the street and make it in Special Forces! I know because I've been through Special Forces Selection, and didn't make it," said the in-processing Army Sergeant. The Sergeant said it couldn't be done, but I did it. I was not alone, either, because there were other outstanding honorable men going down this same path. It was not long after the 9/11 tragedy when I decided to enlist in the military like many other patriotic Americans. I decided to get educated on the military, did my research, and figured out where I wanted to be. I wanted to be a Special Forces Green Beret, and was able to make it happen having and using *The Asset Mindset*.

How did I do this, and why do I believe so strongly in *The Asset Mindset?* I was born in the mid-1970s, with an unknown path ahead of me just like everyone else. I grew up learning about life day to day, and year by year through my experiences. I observed many things as I aged, and didn't realize during these instances that I was learning and creating a certain mindset. As time went by I started to notice themes in life and in myself that led to great success in achieving my goals. I have been able to overcome great challenges achieving goals that others have believed or would believe were impossible. While in my teens, I won multiple martial arts tournaments which included two National Championships, without even realizing I was using *The Asset Mindset* at the time.

Later, while using *The Asset Mindset,* I became a U.S. Army soldier and one of the very few to become an elite Special Forces Green Beret. Even after leaving active duty with the Special Forces, I found myself in surreal situations working for and befriending celebrities thanks to *The Asset Mindset.* I have been fortunate to travel the world making so many of my different dreams come true. Some of these dreams I would have also deemed impossible if it was not for the positivity of *The Asset Mindset* that I built within myself. We all build and create our mindsets, either positively or negatively, and continue to do so throughout our lives. *The Asset Mindset* is the positive means that enables me to achieve success in my life, and it can be your means as well.

Now, this book is not all about me. It is more of a "How to" book that will teach you how to use your mind as your greatest asset. It will have some stories from my life experiences, but the book is really about being a motivational tool for you! Your own personal development--learning, growing, expansion, making positive choices in your life, and becoming your own greatest asset for yourself--these are the key themes of this book. I will help show you the way with some of my experiences, along with experiences of some truly amazing people who I have been blessed to have accompanied me during my life's journey. There are many common themes that are shared by successful people, from elite military special operators, rock stars, world class athletes, and business people alike. They have what I call and deem *The Asset Mindset* philosophy.

There are some exceptional stories in this book which come from the Special Forces community, and soldiers with whom I have been blessed to serve. Words cannot express enough what an honor and pleasure it was, and still is to call these men my brothers. Many of their stories and experiences have completely humbled me as a man, especially the many stories that *can't* be shared in this book. When reflecting on how I got to be associated with this caliber of people with their magnificent spirits, big hearts, and incredible honor, the simple fact is that it reflects on the greatest love of fellow man. They are more than willing to sacrifice for their fellow man in the most horrid of conditions, and even give their lives to protect the ones they love. Our stories will be used to explain, teach, and motivate you to create *The Asset Mindset* in yourself.

This book will teach, guide, and explain to you how it works. It will direct what you can do to create your own *Asset Mindset*, apply it to your own goals, and create success in anything you want to do. This book is written to be direct, get right to the root of problems, and not waste time with lots of fluff. I'm not going to try and impress you with fancy words or lots of long-winded stories, because this book is about making changes and getting results. It's how we Special Operators like to do things, although admittedly sometimes we are definitely guilty of getting long-winded with our stories when we get together. It is *highly* recommended you prepare to take some notes or keep a journal when reading this book as an aid in establishing your own *Asset Mindset* philosophy. In summary, having *The Asset Mindset* is to take ownership of yourself, to overcome difficult situations, always pursue your goals, and strive to be successful in your life in any type of situation. It is the "How to" mindset for creating a successful, and fulfilling life. Are you ready?

Chapter 1

How to Overcome Obstacles

A young man stood in the open door of a C-130 aircraft, wind howling, engines roaring, jumpmaster yelling, thousands of feet in the air. Scared to death, he was the number one jumper, with fear in his eyes and tears rolling down his flushed cheeks, preparing to jump for the very first time. This was a huge personal obstacle for this young soldier wanting to become a Paratrooper. As the number two jumper during this initial jump at Airborne School, I had a front row seat to this extremely intense life event, and his fear and doubt were palpable. He asked to change spots, and my response was, "Sure, but only if the Jumpmaster will let you trade with me." Of course, the Jumpmaster completely denied this request, following it up with yelling a 30 second warning. Then the green light to start jumping came on, and the jumpmaster screamed, *"Go, Go, GO!"* The number one man, completely scared to death with the tears now flowing down his face, was thinking this could be the end of his life. But still, I watched him take his leap into the vast emptiness of the blue sky.

Depending on our own experiences and perspectives on dealing with fear and doubt, this initial jump event might or might not have been much of an obstacle for you. Then again, this situation may be something we can all relate to on some level. No matter where we are on the spectrum, every person in this world faces obstacles at one time or another which fill us with fear and doubt. It is how we take on and face these obstacles that sets us up for success. We can freeze up, do nothing, and get nowhere. This freeze up situation could be related to a job, personal relationship, or even where we live. Many people are stuck in their life circumstances because they don't know what to do, or are just too scared to do anything. This is the worst possible situation. Do not do this! Developing *The Asset Mindset* will keep us from making this mistake in life, because if we are frozen, we cannot grow. There is a saying in the military, that "Not making a decision is the worst possible decision you can make!" This translates into: if you are not doing something, or you're "frozen" on the battlefield, then it's only a matter of time until the enemy will move in on you, and you will lose. By the same token, don't be frozen in life. Do not let time and the world move in on you. We must get past the life obstacles which cause fear and doubt if we truly desire to have success.

Ideally, we all know that overcoming an obstacle is the best way to obtain success, and having *The Asset Mindset* will make this a possibility for us. Instead of freezing up and retreating by going backwards, a better choice is to go forward and overcome. This doesn't mean we can never go backwards to gather some momentum. Sometimes, going backwards allows us to gain the energy in order to move beyond an obstacle, or maybe even around the obstacle in your life. The key is that you need to be doing *something*. DO SOMETHING! Go over, go under, go around, or go through the obstacle. Do whatever it takes to get past the obstacle that stands in the way of achieving your goal. If not, you will be stuck. If we are not actively making decisions to overcome or get around an obstacle in front of us, then nothing will change for us. As we say in the military, "adapt, improvise, and overcome." The important thing is that we have *The Asset Mindset*, keep making moves, and find a way past whatever obstacle we may be facing in our lives.

The US Army Special Forces has the motto "De Oppresso Liber," which is displayed on our Special Forces crest. This motto means, "To liberate from oppression." It is also commonly interpreted as, "To free the oppressed." This is the Green Berets' core mission statement in the operations we conduct all around the world every day. It is also something that can be adapted to be used in one's personal mindset. Many people oppress themselves with their own negative thoughts and ways of thinking. We need to take on this motto and apply it to ourselves when creating *The Asset Mindset* within us. Free your mind of negative thoughts. Do not oppress yourself in your mind. Make it a mission statement in your life and in your head, so that you can free yourself from oppressive thinking. Have awareness of your mind, and free your mind in such a way that you create positive changes in your whole thought process. We need to build ourselves up in our minds in such a way that we realize we are amazing, and can achieve greatness along with success. It is possible. If this is something you struggle with, then you need to seek out help from others who are positive assets. They will lift you up mentally, and be on your side or team. This will be covered in even greater detail later on we discuss *Asset Mindset* teammates. No matter what, do not allow yourself to be an oppressor of your own mind. Free your mind of oppression, and you will have the foundation for developing *The Asset Mindset* .

Gratitude is a tremendously powerful tool that we can use to overcome oppression, or negativity, in our own minds. Whenever we feel down, or feel things are not what we want, we must take a moment to look around and think of three things that we are grateful for. For example, you may be grateful for your family, friends, pets, food, or health. This becomes extremely forceful when combating negativity in our minds. We all seem to get distracted sometimes, thinking that we still have so far to go, which can be very discouraging. When this happens to you, stop for a moment. Look back, and see how far you have traveled. Have gratitude for what you have achieved, and be grateful for where you currently are in life. Gratitude is probably the most effective tool that we can use to overcome the oppression of a negative mind.

Furthermore, it is very important to be grateful for what we already have. A person owning an old beat up car may look at someone with a shiny new one and feel inadequate, along with feeling negatively about themselves. Yet, the person walking along the road may look at the old beat up car and feel inferior, because they don't even own a car. Then there is a sick person laying in their bed gazing out the window viewing the person walking along the road, wishing they felt better so they could go for a walk along the road. Meanwhile, there is a seriously ill person laying in a hospital bed wishing they could just go home and be in their own bed. By now, you should get the point. Be grateful for what you have and where you are, because things can always be worse. The most wonderful thing about gratitude is that the more we think about it, and the more we have it, the happier we are. We just can't help it. It's pretty simple, really; just as the more water we drink, the more hydrated we become, and the better we feel, gratitude works the same way; the more we invite it into our lives, the happier we become. It is a tool which definitely enables us to create a better mindset.

You may be wondering what ever happened to the number one man who jumped from the airplane. Well, after I followed him out of the aircraft and watched him land safely on the ground, he came up to me and said, "I'm sorry for the way I acted up there." It was obvious he was quite embarrassed about what had just transpired. My reaction was not what he expected. "I was really very impressed by your actions," I responded. He looked back at me, perplexed. I then began to explain what my interpretation of the events was. I knew he was scared to death, but I got to watch him display true courage, and see a man overcome his fear. He may have been scared with tears in his eyes, but he jumped out of the C-130 all on his own, without the forced assistance of the Airborne Instructor. He made his choice and took action to jump; to go after his goal to become Airborne qualified. You see, in the US Army's Airborne School, there are no jump refusals once you board the aircraft. The time to quit is before you board the aircraft, which many soldiers do. If you board the aircraft, you understand you are saying you are willing to jump, even if the Black Hats (Airborne Instructors) have to kick you out of the aircraft's door. This initial jump was a solid example of a powerful mindset. He was going to overcome his fear of jumping and potentially dying, no matter what. The fear inside him gave him an opportunity to be courageous, brave, and have a shining moment. I was lucky enough to witness it firsthand. Jumper one graduated from Airborne School, and proudly went off to serve with the 82nd Airborne Division at Fort Bragg. Remember, fear is an opportunity to display courage. Be courageous in your life, and people will take notice.

Let's talk more about fear, what it is, and how it affects our lives. To start, everyone is afraid of something. If someone says they never feel fear, then they are just lying to us and to themselves. According to Merriam-Webster dictionary, fear is: "An unpleasant, often strong emotion caused by anticipation or awareness of danger. This danger can be and most often is associated with physical harm or being hurt." Nevertheless, we all know that we can be emotionally or mentally hurt, as well. This fear is where anxiety can rear its ugly head and make an obstacle seem even more difficult to deal with. The bravest people I know experience fear, and are afraid of things. They also have *The Asset Mindset*: to face the effects of fear head on, to be courageous, and to overcome their fear. We can do this, too, by understanding fear and strengthening our mindsets.

Only you are in control of your mindset. As you continue to journey through this book and your life, you will have opportunities to learn to make positive changes in your mindset, just like the number one man did on his first jump. You want to be courageous, bold, and brave in life, right? Well, you need to make a choice to act. If you act, guess what? You will be able to achieve all those things, but you have to recognize that fear is going to be present when you do so! Fear is not a bad thing. Fear is an opportunity to grow and do something great; don't let it stop you! Fear is an obstacle that can be overcome. People are doing just that every minute of every day. We must seize the moment and all our future moments to come. More often than not, when there is no risk, there is no reward. Sometimes, the greatest rewards are associated with the greatest risks and fears. Get your mindset to see fear as an opportunity to grow and to be brave, amazing, and powerful-- because that is the reality of your true potential.

This does not mean that our fear should be completely ignored. It is there for a reason; it is a primal emotion that humans experience. Our fears and gut feelings are most likely warranted, and should be listened to while we exercise good judgement using *The Asset Mindset*. For example, we should be afraid to jump out of a C-130 without a parachute, so let's make sure we have one. Fears should not automatically be ignored; they need to be understood. You have to learn to recognize the difference between a fear that is warranted (jumping out of an airplane without a parachute) and a fear that is holding you back (being afraid to jump with a parachute and all necessary safety precautions in place). Once you understand your fears, you can address them and overcome them appropriately using *The Asset Mindset*.

Understand that making progress or growth can be painful at times, but do not let it be an obstacle that stops you. We must move through the pain to make progress. Growth can be mentally painful, such as the loss of a loved one when a relationship goes bad, or physically painful, like the day after a hard workout in the gym. There is also the next-level stuff, like a woman giving birth to a child. Obviously, this is serious pain, but it is not a bad thing. Women who go through birthing often refer to it as a blessing, and say that going through the experience makes them grow as a person. In whatever form they take, growing pains are real, but they are yet another obstacle that can be overcome if we have the right mindset. We need to understand that growth is commonly associated with some sort of pain. Focusing on the positive outcome of growth instead of the painful growth process is one way to endure and overcome it. Even if it is bad pain, it is just another obstacle that every single person has to face at different points. Things happen in life, and it's not the pain that defines who we become in the future. It's how we choose to let the pain shape our lives after the fact that is truly important. Remember: you are not alone when it comes to dealing with pain. People are overcoming painful obstacles in their lives and growing through the process every single day. Obstacles like pain most definitely can and will be overcome with a strong positive mindset.

Next, let's look at doubt. Doubt is one of the biggest obstacles that I see people facing all the time in life, and one of the things some of our current youth seem to be really struggling with. We have all heard someone or a child say, "I can't do it!" Doubt is probably one of the most dangerous obstacles out there, because if you do not think you can do something, then most likely you never will. Even worse, doubt can also lead to quitting, and if you quit you will absolutely 100% not achieve your goal. Do not let doubt make you quit. Just think of a baby learning to walk. When a baby first tries to walk and fails, do they give up and let doubt take over, acting like they can't walk? Do they quit? Never! Otherwise, we would all still be crawling around on our hands and knees well into adulthood. Well, come to think of it, there is lots of crawling around as an adult in the military. But that's not the type of crawling that we are talking about here. The point is, if a young baby can overcome doubt and fear, then you can overcome these feelings, too!

We may never know exactly why babies overcome and continue to push themselves to walk, because they don't have the ability to tell us. An interesting theory to consider is that they are motivated to walk because they are constantly surrounded by other human beings who are walking upright. We are showing them what is possible. Undoubtedly, this is a huge influence on them, and may demonstrate the power that people in our environment have to show us what we can achieve. Remember: these ideas about our environment, who we are surrounded by, and their power to influence us in ways that are both positive and negative, as it will come up again. The key points for overcoming doubt are that we need to focus on our goals, believe in ourselves and our dreams, or they will not happen. Believing and beliefs will be topics discussed in much greater detail later. As for right now, understand that we need to eliminate the obstacle of doubt from our mindsets and from our goals. Whether we think we can or think we can't, we will be right!

A perfect example of overcoming doubt and using a mindset to overcome obstacles is my mother, Maryellen. At the age of thirty-seven, she faced a major tragedy when she suffered from a stroke followed by serious internal infections. This ordeal resulted in the loss of more than half a lung, along with lots of other complications which included becoming mostly paralyzed on her left side. Wheelchair bound and leaving the hospital, she was told by her doctors that she would not be able to walk again, and that her life expectancy was no higher than fifty-five. Still, my mother was undaunted; she would not allow the doubt placed in her head by the doctors to become an obstacle that limited her life. There were copious amounts of pain and lots of tears, but she spent countless hours in rehabilitation, maintaining a strong mindset pushing herself forward. All of her hard work produced results, and she was able to achieve the ability to walk again.

As time passed, her health continued to be an obstacle in life, as she went on to endure a serious car accident where her neck was broken, and a breast cancer diagnosis which led to a mastectomy. All of these challenges caused her to spend months in the hospital, and even more time in rehabilitation. Despite these major setbacks, she always chose to push forward. My mother would always say, "I have so much to live for," and "I need to stick around for my family." This love for life and her family was the fuel she always used to drive her mindset to recovery. It was the reason she fought so hard. Find your love, and your own reason(s) to fuel your mindset. Mom would always appreciate even the littlest things that showed improvement in her recoveries. Each and every little advancement she made gave her confidence that she could achieve more. These small things empowered her and reinforced her positive beliefs that she was in control and could change her situations for the better.

It was a long and labored process at times, but every little bit of progress added up to bring her to where she is today. She has pushed so long, and so hard that at the time of writing this book, my mother is now a decade past the life expectancy the doctors gave her! The best part is that she's still pushing, and who knows how far her love and mindset will take her. Your love and your mindset are the greatest assets to overcoming your challenges and achieving your goals. We can all overcome obstacles and doubt when we apply a strong positive mindset, allowing ourselves to achieve what seemed impossible to even the so-called experts.

We have discussed the mental obstacles of fear and doubt, but there are also the emotional and physical obstacles that people have to deal with. These mainly stem from environmental problems or physical difficulties. Guess what, though? You are a human being, and human beings have this amazing ability to change the environment around them! Whatever you are currently facing may seem like the biggest obstacle ever for you to overcome, but that is an *illusion*. Do not let your mind trick you into making excuses for yourself, or justify the thinking that your obstacles are insurmountable. People run without legs! Read without sight! Fly without wings! People even love after a broken heart. The truth of the matter is that people can overcome any obstacle with the right mindset, motivation, and effort. If you have any physical, emotional, or environmental problems you are dealing with, know that you can overcome them by making wise choices, taking decisive action, and having a positive mindset. You can do it, and you are already doing it by reading this book.

Chapter 2

Where to Begin

It was zero dark thirty in the morning with a thick soupy fog. Our friend Bob, commonly referenced as the bright sun in the military community, was just coming out to burn the fog off for another scorching hot and humid summer day in North Carolina. We had approximately 50 miles to cover on foot in three days, while each carrying at least 55 pounds on our backs. It was going to be one hell of a trek, with mental and physical obstacles all along the way. Where to begin? How to tackle such a challenge? We began mentally by focusing on our overall purpose and aspirations, well before we received the orders to take on this long arduous trek. Our tentative plan was created next, and then we acted, taking our first steps off in the direction and route we wanted to take. All the while, we were completely unaware of what laid before us.

Why mention this journey, you might be wondering? Well, this is a small example of what life is. You are currently on your own personal trek or journey, and who knows what lays ahead of you. Are you ready to take the steps that will carry you in the direction you want to go?

The first thing we need to do in establishing *The Asset Mindset* is take some time for ourselves and get ourselves prepared mentally. Get educated and learn things that will help you in your journey. Congratulations, because you are doing one of those things right now while reading. Spend time in your mind thinking about what to do, how to do it, where do you want to go, and what do you want to be. For motivation, think about your "why." Why do you want to do the thing that you're doing? Write things down, journal, make lists, use a dry erase white board, and get organized! The more we feel organized, the more control we will have, and the easier our lives will be. We don't want to be wandering on our life trek aimlessly. Get focused on your thoughts, and if they are not positive or if they don't coincide with your goals, don't focus on them. Organization is crucial to getting ourselves mentally focused and prepared.

You may have heard of the old Cherokee legend about a grandfather teaching his grandson about life. "A fight is going on inside me," he told the boy. "It is a terrible fight, and it is between two wolves. One wolf is evil or negative and is anger, envy, sorrow, regret, greed, arrogance, self-pity, guilt, resentment, inferiority, lies, false pride, superiority, and ego. The other wolf is good or positive, and he is full of joy, peace, love, hope, serenity, humility, kindness, benevolence, empathy, generosity, truth, compassion, and faith. The same fight is going on inside you, and inside of everyone else too."

The young grandson asked his grandfather, "Which wolf will win?" The grandfather replied, "The one you feed!" Get your mindset right for your life journey, and feed your mind with positive thoughts.

Part of being mentally prepared is believing in ourselves. We need to stop comparing ourselves to others, and be the best version of ourselves. It doesn't matter what others are doing; it matters what *we* are doing. We need to believe in ourselves, and be willing to invest time and effort into ourselves. Feed the parts of yourself and your dreams that you want to come true. You are a creator, so start creating the things you desire. This is where we must start when taking on any challenge or journey in our lives. Do not limit yourself, or worry too much about where you are in your life journey right now. To better understand this point, there is a great quote by motivational speaker and businessman, Nido Qubein: "Your present circumstances don't determine where you can go; they merely determine where you start." Understanding these concepts, building your mental preparedness, and your belief in yourself is an absolute key part of *The Asset Mindset.* We will broach this topic again in greater detail later on, and more than once. For now, just remember that these three key things allow us to properly start to prepare for the future: mental preparedness, the proper beliefs, and mindset.

Motivation is also extremely important. It is the fire that will help fuel our actions to obtain our life's goals or overcome any obstacles on our journey.

Learn what gets you motivated, and work on it. Find your passion. If your motivation is low, we have a saying in the military: "False motivation is better than no motivation." In more modern or civilian slang, I have heard, "Fake it till you make it." I don't want you to be a fake, but at times when you are at a low point, just acting as if you were really motivated will help you, and even encourage others around you to become more motivated. I have done and witnessed this happen countless times in life, and it truly works. There is even scientific evidence to support this type of concept. Research by psychologists has shown that if you're unhappy, just fake a smile, because the act of physically smiling can force your mind to literally be happy! Your mind reacts, registering to itself, "I'm smiling; I must be happy." When this occurs, a happier mindset will actually start to follow. Motivation or false motivation work the same way on your mind.

We need to search ourselves and our minds to find what motivates us. Once you find it, grab a hold of it tight, never let go, and use it every day, because motivation is an amazingly powerful asset. Just like author Zig Ziglar famously stated, "People often say that motivation doesn't last. Well neither does bathing- that's why we recommend it daily." When we are and stay properly motivated while working towards success, we will be taking our first step towards having *The Asset Mindset.*

Next comes discipline. The more we have, the more likely we are to have success. Discipline is like the glue that holds everything together. People get great ideas and are motivated all the time; New Year's resolutions are a perfect example of this, but even just watching a movie or reading a good book can do it. What good is all that motivation if you don't have the discipline to keep it going, though? This is probably one of the most difficult, or is the most difficult thing for people to do. It requires changing behaviors and real effort on our part. We can have all these wonderful goals, desires, and motivations, but if we don't have the discipline to work on them daily, then they most likely won't ever happen.

We need to really want it. We need to grow up, we need to make plans, and we need to work our plans with discipline every single day. You can do this by making a schedule and giving yourself deadlines for certain tasks.

Get a calendar and mark it up, be modern and use your smartphone, or draw something out by hand; just do whatever it takes for you to get it done, and stick to it! Make yourself accountable, and tell people about your plans. This will aid you in staying on track. When others ask you, "How's your plan coming along?" or ask about your plan in general, you will want to have answers for them when they do. Every successful person I have come across, from famous musicians, actors, athletes, and of course warriors from the Special Operations community, have had the discipline to get themselves to where they wanted to be. They worked for it, and we will have to work for it as well. As the Buddha is said to have stated, "The person who masters himself through self-control and discipline is truly undefeatable." The more discipline, or glue these successful people used to hold their plan together, the better and faster it was accomplished. This fact about discipline holds the same truth for us too!

The time to make time an asset is now. Time is one of the strange and mysterious forces that can either work against us or for us, based on how we use it. It tends to move faster and faster as we go through life, yet there are also times when it seems to drag. Our mindset and choices will affect how we see and utilize the time we have. The important thing with time is that we need to truly realize it is a limited asset, but also a very powerful asset. We only have so much, so it needs to be used wisely. The sooner we can appreciate the time we have, and the ability it has to be an asset for us, the better off we will be.

Using time as an asset is a pretty simple concept, but it can be very difficult to do without discipline. For example, let's look at a year time frame. A year can go by pretty fast, and most likely will be over before we know it. Having the mindset to use our time wisely can make large tasks or problems much easier to accomplish. For example, writing a book or novel can seem like a daunting task. However, using proper discipline along with using time as an asset properly, just by writing a single page a day, you can have a 365-page novel in a year. Another example is weight loss. If people who want to lose weight could commit themselves to losing a single pound per week, they could lose 52 pounds in a year. That is like losing a large travel suitcase, fully packed! Have the mindset where you understand that the time to begin working toward your goals is now. Follow this by staying disciplined with your efforts, and you will see that time will become an amazing asset and act as a force multiplier. The time to make time your asset is now!

Chapter 3

What to Avoid: Environments, People, and Excuses

"Let's get the hell out of here!"

We were all caught completely off guard; one minute, we had just been partying having a great time in a motel room, and the next second, this crazy guy burst in the room yelling like a maniac.

Someone exclaimed; "Why? What happened?"

"The manager just called the cops when he caught me breaking into the motel's office safe," he replied. Panicked, people downed their drinks and started grabbing their stuff .

Somebody else responded, "Really! Are you serious?"

We thought he was just trying to mess with everyone by pulling a prank at the motel party. However, he definitely wasn't as he ran out the front door frantically telling everyone, "Let's go now!" *You've got to be kidding me,* I thought to myself. *What a stupid dumbass!*

Everyone rushed out of the motel room and went out to the parking lot, piling into a car to leave. Listening to my gut, I refused to get into the car, saying, "I want nothing to do with this! I am going to walk home."

They called me crazy and gave me a hard time, because it was miles and miles back to my house. Still, I strongly refused, and they took off speeding out of the motel parking lot to get the hell out of there. Less than thirty seconds into my walk up the road, there were sirens screaming and lights flashing as two police cruisers raced by me with a loud *whoosh*. I was in for a very long night of walking, but I just kept moving forward. Eventually, I made it home the next morning.

As it turned out, later that following week, I came across people who had been at the party. They asked what had happened to me. "Nothing really, except for a long and tiring walk," I told them, "What happened to you guys?" They answered that everyone who had left in the car had gotten arrested, and had spent the night in jail. That was why I had seen the police cars go speeding by. It turns out that I had been 100% right to trust my gut and walk home, even if it meant walking all night.

This quick little story of a past experience right after high school highlights in many ways what not to do, what to do, and which environments and people to avoid so as to not affect your life in a negative way. Sometimes, we need to step off on our own and avoid peer pressure in order to do what we feel is the right decision. As we can see from the story, some of those people at the party probably were not the best people to be associated with, especially the guy who was breaking into the motel's office safe. They wanted me to go with them in the car, and gave me a hassle for not wanting to go. What a difference in outcomes from making one smart decision! Choices matter, and some can and will affect you for the rest of your life. Listen to your gut and make the right choices for yourself and your life.

Making the right choices may leave us all alone for a while with a long road ahead of us, but making the right or hard decision will always pay off in the end. Listening to others, getting into that car, and getting arrested after high school may have changed my entire life path. When I was inquiring about joining Special Forces, one of the first questions the Army recruiter asked me was, "Have you ever been arrested?" Thankfully, I was able to answer, "no." Had I not been able to answer, "no," my future goals and military career may have been completely upended. The people and the environment at the motel party were not constructive or positive for my life success. Luckily, I had the right mindset to walk away. When something doesn't sit right with you, don't just go along for the ride or give in to the pressure of others. Stay strong, listen to your gut, and follow your heart. Look out for yourself and be your own greatest asset.

We need to be aware of people who inspire us and make us want to be more successful in life. Stay away from people with a crab mentality, or "crab heads." This references an old Philippine metaphor about crabs in a bucket or pot, which goes something like this. Individually, a crab could easily escape and climb out from the bucket. But instead, when there are other crabs in the bucket, they will grab each other in a useless "king of the hill" competition. This prevents any crab from escaping, and ensures the crabs' collective demise. This same effect can be found in human behavior when members of a group attempt to sabotage any other member who achieves, or is attempting to achieve success beyond the group. This can be based on jealousy, envy, conspiracy, or competitive feelings. It can also be described as, "If I can't have it, then neither can you," type of thinking. Stay away from groups or people like this, and don't let them poison your mind with self-doubt or self-loathing. We need to make it a habit to associate and spend our time with people who inspire us and help us grow.

Let's dig a little deeper into the role that is played by the environment around us. There is always an environment around us that we have to deal with. It's pretty simple to say that we should immerse ourselves in a positive environment, but this is not always a simple or easy thing to do. For example, there are times when we don't even know that we are in a negative environment. These can be environments that we consider normal, have become accustomed to over time, or we have just grown up with, so we don't know any better. We can also be desensitized by an environment, or even indoctrinated into it over a period of time. It's sad to say that many of these environments are occupied by people who supposedly love us, or do not know how to love us properly. These intimate environments are the toughest to break free of, but still it can be done.

I'm going to share an example of someone very inspiring and close to me, so close to me that I married her twice! She has been amazingly successful since breaking free from the abusive and negative environment she was exposed to and grew up in. You see, for years Kimberly just thought that's how things were. People told her she was a dumb blonde and couldn't do certain things. When I first met her, she would even call herself a dumb blonde, but you will *never* ever hear Kimberly say that again! She used to believe the lies that were being put into her head. The environment was extremely negative, very controlling, and the people around her accomplished this by putting her down instead of lifting her up. She was full of self-doubt, and would often make excuses as to why they treated her that way. They would laugh at her and her ideas, preventing her from growing and getting ahead in life.

From our 2nd marriage when we renewed our vows.

So, how did this woman make the changes in her life to break free from this negative environment? The answer is simply that it started with love. Yes, a former Special Forces soldier saying it started with love. We are not just cold-hearted warriors who want to destroy and blow up everything. We just destroy the evil-doers, bad guys, anyone who threatens freedom, and those attacking the innocent people of the world. The true reason Special Operators are so successful is because of *love*: love for our family, brothers in arms, freedom, fellow human beings, and of course, love of country. Now, back to this woman breaking free from her negative environment with the power of love.

It started when Kimberly became the mother of a sweet baby boy who changed her whole life. Those of you who are mothers reading this book know what I am talking about. For those who aren't mothers or fathers, the love of her baby boy made her realize that she didn't want him growing up in the same negative and abusive environment she was currently in, so she left. She could have made excuses in her head for why she was stuck in that environment, but she couldn't justify any excuses for her baby. She stopped making excuses all together, and stepped out onto a new life path, which for her meant walking alone as a single mother for a little while.

While walking on this new path, she began to change her mindset and grow. She was creating an environment inspired by love. This new path was not a quick and easy change. However, it was necessary and *so worth it* for her personal growth and to create a better future. We also have this power and the same opportunity to change our life paths, just as she did. The new environment she created has led her to become the amazing woman that she is today. This once so-called dumb blonde is now a healthcare professional who holds multiple certifications in the medical field. She previously had a negative mindset, but transformed her mindset through love and positivity to the point where she turned her life around and now helps save other people's lives on a regular basis.

Kimberly could have allowed herself to be stuck in a victim mentality by blaming her past mental, emotional, physical, and sexual abuse for all of her problems. There was also an instance when she was kidnapped with a knife held at her throat when she was just sixteen years old, barely escaping with her life. Her attacker was found guilty after the offense and sentenced to 15-30 years in prison. That extremely violent event alone could have been used as a crutch or excuse for the rest of her life. Actually, any one of these different past traumatic events could have easily been used as an excuse for being a victim for the rest of her life. She had multiple reasons to blame negative people, her past experiences, and past environments as excuses for being stuck in a bad situation and not getting ahead in life, but she didn't do that. Everyone, including you, has reasons they can use as excuses to stay stuck in a bad place in life. Some reasons make for bigger or stronger excuses, and others less so. Yet, when it comes right down to it, no matter how weak or strong your excuses are, it is all still just allowing yourself to be a victim. *Do not* allow yourself to be stuck in a victim mentality.

While people can victimize us in life, they cannot keep us in a victim mentality. This is very important to understand, and cannot be overemphasized. You cannot control what happens to you in life, but whether or not you fall into a victim's mindset is 100%, completely up to you. Be an asset to yourself like she was, and do not allow yourself to be a victim. A negative experience from our past is just an event that has happened to us; *it does not define us!* It is something to learn from and to become stronger for having gone through it.

My Green Beret brother Ryan Hendrickson, who came back from nearly having his leg blown off by an IED to later earn a Silver Star in combat, states it powerfully in his book 'Tip of the Spear' when he writes, "I choose to set the rules of my life and not let the memories of the past haunt me and dictate my future." Breaking victim mentality is a must! Seek out help from others, or help from professionals, if you feel you need assistance with this. We cannot have and use *The Asset Mindset* if we feel like a victim. Being a victim means we have given over control of our lives to someone, something, or some event in our lives. *The Asset Mindset* is the total opposite of this. It puts us and our minds in control of our lives allowing us to focus on the road ahead of us. You are in the driver's seat taking your life in the direction you want it to go. Drive wisely and own your life.

Kimberly's change in mindset did not happen overnight, so don't be discouraged if it takes you some time to evolve, as well. Just keep working it and you *will* get results. Unconditional love was the spark that started the fire inside her, but it took a while to burn through all of the negative people in her life, her abusive past, and the excuses that were obstacles in her way.

Once love became a priority, Kimberly made another important discovery. She began to notice the difference between the people in her life who were truly loving and the fake people who always had conditions attached to their love. This fake love was a control mechanism that was used on her. The actions of these people would tell her, "Do, say, and act as you're told, and you will be loved." If this technique is used on us, or if it is a part of our environment, we must be very cautious when dealing with these people. If this situation sounds familiar to you, recognize that a guilt technique is being used as a control mechanism just like it was used on Kimberly. People trying to control and manipulate her would say, "We did this for you in the past, so you need to do what we want in return now." Ask yourself, "What are these people's motives?" Are they using this to control you for their own benefit? It is important to be savvy and aware if you find yourself in this situation.

Now, do also recognize that there is such a thing as tough love, like not giving money to a gambler or not giving a drink to a drunk. That is why we must look at the person's motives, and see if they are being selfish or loving. A loving person or environment will always push us in a positive direction, and support us to become the best person we can be. They won't hold us back, or put up with any of our excuses either. If anything, they will kick us in the behind and say "Get going on those positive changes in your life!" Change doesn't happen overnight. However, we can make change happen with the right mindset.

This incredible woman did not start off with *The Asset Mindset*, but with time and effort she was able to learn and create it for herself. Her story and growth reflect a major point in this book, which is that you do NOT need to be Special Forces to have *The Asset Mindset*. You can have it, create it, and apply it in your life no matter who you are and what your background is. Kimberly realized that her problems from the past did not define her future. Today, she says: "When you're in a bad situation, you may not realize how influential a person or people can be on your mind. They can have a profound impact on your psyche without you even realizing it. If you don't have enough positivity in your life, you may be missing out on your fullest potential. Do some soul searching, create a positive mindset, surround yourself with positive people, and determine what type of people you want influencing your life."

Kimberly today has a professional medical career that she never thought she could achieve, and has created her dream home full of positivity and love with acres of land across from a mountain resort. How inspiring! The amazing thing is, she is not done yet, and she is still laser focused on creating even more dreams for the future. She lives with *The Asset Mindset* every day now, and is a doer. It is going to be exciting to see where Kimberly goes next. Take inspiration from her story. You too can learn and create your own *Asset Mindset* if you don't fully have one yet, because you control your focus. We can't allow ourselves to make excuses or let our environments control us. The time and effort we put into creating *The Asset Mindset* will undoubtedly create positive results.

Excuses are very dangerous. Be extremely leery of excuses, both our own and the ones that others will give us. Recalling the quote by Howard Wright, "Excuses are lies wrapped up in reasons." A prime example of this is, "I wanted to work out today, but I was too tired." The truth of the matter is that if you really want something, you are going to do it whether you are tired or not. Another excuse would be, "I am not smart enough," or "I don't know how." These are things we commonly tell ourselves in order to avoid hard work and challenges in life. Instead of letting yourself believe these lies, push yourself to get out there and learn. Get smarter so that you *can* know how or what to do. We live in an age where you can learn just about anything with the push of a button on a computer, or smartphone. Answers are everywhere, so there is no good excuse. It is never too late to grow and improve the quality of your life. There is always something we can do at any stage of our lives. We have all heard of the stories of the eighty-something-year-old finally getting their high school diploma or college degree. Our goals can be achieved, so let's not make excuses. If we find ourselves or people around us making excuses, we need to confront it. It's not easy to confront others--or even ourselves, for that matter--but it needs to be done for any progress to be made. In the Special Forces community, people get called out immediately if somebody tries to use an excuse. We all know that excuses are hazardous, and they are a danger to us and our goals, so as a community we all share the mindset to not buy into excuses.

These excuses, or this negative mindset, leads into the "I can't" mentality. When you think of your dreams and goals, do you think, "I can't do that" or "I can do that?" If you already believe you can do it, then wonderful! You are well on your way to living your life with *The Asset Mindset*. However, if you are like lots of other people who are not quite there at the present moment, here is an *Asset Mindset* technique you should use to become a better asset for yourself. Start thinking, "How do I?" Thinking "How do I" instead of "I can't" will change your whole perspective in life. This type of thinking will give us another piece of the puzzle for having *The Asset Mindset*.

This key feature of *The Asset Mindset* is also a fundamental aspect of how Special Operations teams get the job done. If we give any wild, crazy, seemingly impossible, and extremely dangerous mission to any Special Operations Team, they won't say, "Oh, we can't." They will simply find a way to get the mission accomplished. If they lived with an "I can't" mentality, then they would be the wrong ones for the job. When I was in the Special Forces and we received an outrageous mission, we always asked ourselves, "Okay, this seems crazy impossible, but how do we do this?" Ask yourself the how, and break it down. Think about the how. Plan the how! This is a great time to exercise some backwards planning techniques which we will cover in greater detail later on. Have *The Asset Mindset* "How do I" mentality, and figure it out! Don't be afraid to ask for help from friends and family who are positive assets in your life if you need it.

Now, let's get back to our environment and the people in it. Take a hard look at yourself and the people you are surrounded by. Are they talkers, or are they doers? This will help us realize whether our time and effort should be spent with them, and in that environment. Lots of people just talk, talk, talk about what they did, what they want to do, and what they could do, but how many of them are actually doing something to pursue what they are saying? Are you pursuing the things you talk about? Are you a "talker" or a "doer?" Spend some time with that, and it will help shed light on your environment and the people in it.

Not to be mistaken, people who "do" also talk about their dreams, plans, and what they have done in the past. This is a good thing when done in a positive light. However, "doers" will support the talk with actions, and are *doing* what they say. This is a great indicator for the people and the environment we want to be in. Avoid people and environments where it is all talk no action. This goes back to my first hero and mentor, my dad, who would tell me, "Don't just talk the talk; you need to walk the walk." Start doing instead of just saying, and really listen to yourself talk. Are you doing what you are saying? If not, then get to it, and start acting on your desires.

Here is a quick story about acting on your desires instead of just talking about them. We were on a large-scale raid partnered with a regular army unit, because we needed their support for blocking positions in a large village. The mission was a success. We got the bad guys, and it was time to return to base. Well, wouldn't you know that Murphy's Law poked his ugly head up. A soldier supporting us accidentally backed his vehicle off the three feet embankment on the side of the road, and got it stuck; like, really stuck, because he kept pushing on the gas and digging it in while trying to get out. That truck was dug into the ground like a crab digs into the sand at the beach. When we heard this over the radio, our team went over to help. When we arrived at their position, everyone was talking about how it was totally stuck and couldn't get out. The embankment was just too high, and the truck was dug in too deep.

They talked about the problem from every angle, but ultimately they decided that it just couldn't be done. The final plan that they had settled on was to send a radio call for help and wait all night for a helicopter to come to their rescue by sling loading their truck, in order to lift it up and out.

As a Special Forces A-Team or Operational Detachment Alpha (ODA), after listening to this helpless debate, we decided to step in. We weren't going to just stand there and talk about the stuck vehicle. We told them to wait on calling for a helicopter because we would get it out, and then we got to work. First, we set up security around their vehicle and then literally dug into the embankment with the few hand tools we had. The regular Army guys at first were saying, "You guys are crazy. You will never get that out by hand!" I recall looking over at a young soldier saying, "Watch us."

Our ODA was a team of doers, and we attacked that embankment like a dog would attack a T-bone steak. Dirt and rocks went flying all over the place. Sweat was pouring out of us like a freshly squeezed orange. Next thing you know, we were making progress, and we got the truck to move a little. The funny thing was, the guys that were at first watching and talking about how it couldn't be done saw what we were accomplishing, and before long they started believing it could be done. Then they even got in on the action, too! It was not easy, and it took us almost two hours of back breaking labor to finish the job, but we got it out by hand, and everyone made it safely back to base that night--minus the need for a helicopter.

This was a great example of different mindsets from different environments, and talking vs. doing. Don't get me wrong; we love our regular army brothers and sisters to death, and they do accomplish amazing things. However, as a whole, they just don't have the same type of training, experience, and mindset as a Special Forces A-Team does. This story is also a great example of how doing something in front of others who believe something can't be done, can show them the possibilities of what can be done and change their beliefs. This is similar to the example of a baby learning to walk, which we discussed previously. Babies know that walking is possible because they see other humans doing it, so they never give up trying until they figure it out! It is extraordinarily powerful for people to be able to see what is possible. Halfway into getting the truck out, everyone who was talking about how it couldn't be done had actually changed their mindset and believed that it *could* be accomplished. A positive mindset can be very contagious. When working to get the vehicle unstuck a few of the regular Army soldiers even started talking about how they were now thinking about going into Special Forces.

Moral of the story is: less talking, more doing, and don't listen to anybody who says that you can't. Just do your thing, and get it done. You do you and you most likely will inspire someone else to step up their game and accomplish something, too!

Let's think of the mind as a sponge. If you drop a dry sponge into a dirty mud puddle, it's going to soak up all of the filthy water. The mind works the same way when it is exposed to a negative environment! On the other hand, if our sponge is already full with clean water or positivity, even when we drop it into a poor environment like a muddy puddle, when we pick it up it will not be nearly as dirty because it is much harder for the impurities to penetrate into the clean waterlogged sponge. In other words, if our brains are already full with a positive mindset, then it is much harder for negative situations or environments to infiltrate and bring us down. Fill your mind with positivity and don't buy into excuses, negative people, or negative environments. If we are ever in a situation where we find ourselves dealing with these issues, we just need to stay focused on being "doers." *The Asset Mindset* will enable us to accomplish this while shining a light for others to see their own potential as well.

Chapter 4

Influences and How to Grow

In the middle of a dense forest, I was attempting to keep up and follow a large six-foot 2-inch Viking of a man so I wouldn't get lost. He was breaking all the brush out of our way with what appeared to be arms and hands made of steel, easily snapping branches as we went along. I asked, "What are we doing?"

His reply was serious and very direct: "Watch and learn, son." I can still hear that voice in my head today. I actually hear that voice all the time. You see, that voice was from Guy Fielding, my father. I was blessed with one hell of a father. He was my teacher, mentor, and first hero, and he helped me grow to levels I couldn't even begin to comprehend when I was a young boy. My father must have told me a million times, "Watch and learn." Just a boy, I would constantly ask him, "Why?" or "What are we doing?" But indeed, I learned from watching his example, and he taught me to learn, grow, and build the foundations for a positive mindset. My father instinctively knew that this was the way to be successful in life. He taught me about drive, and working hard for what you want, saying things like, "You can do anything if you work hard enough, son--and most of all, don't quit!"

Little did I know then just how much my father's words would come to mean to me later in life as I was creating *The Asset Mindset* and serving as a Special Forces Green Beret. Another motivational dad quote worth sharing comes from my Green Beret brother Ryan Hendrickson, author of *Tip of the Spear*[1], where he quoted his father saying, "If you don't try, you will never know, and if you don't know, it's because you didn't try." There is nothing more valuable to help you grow than the words of a mentor who loves you, so reflect and think back on yours often. My father mentored me with his words and actions so that it actually made the mental part of becoming a

Green Beret not so difficult. He is the main reason I am the man I am today. Thankfully, I watched and learned.

Work ethic was and still is so important to accomplishing goals. My father taught me to work hard in all conditions; cold, wet, hungry, and tired. Honestly, as a boy I was quite distraught with him at times for this. I am sure my son feels the exact same way with me when I try to teach him about having a strong work ethic, but I love him too much to not pass it on. This solid work ethic came in extremely handy later on in life, especially while in the Special Forces, and it still helps me everyday to accomplish my tasks.

My father was a builder, master carpenter, and an old school badass working man who did pretty much everything himself. He fixed and worked on everything, from houses to vehicles. You name it, and he did it with me as his little sidekick, watching and learning. With all the problems and obstacles that come up in everyday life, he showed me day in and day out that they can be overcome with hard work. I watched and learned, discovering along the way that it wasn't always going to be easy. It is no exaggeration to say that there was literally blood, sweat, and tears in the Fielding household on a regular basis. Nonetheless, our home was also filled with tremendous amounts of love, laughter, and celebration when things were accomplished. There was a sense of accomplishment and pride that comes from being able to overcome an obstacle through your own hard work.

Me and my dad, who is my mentor and my 1st hero.

Having a strong work ethic allows us to accomplish things that other people view as impossible. A great example of this is an experience that I had around age 12. My dad and I had spent a Friday afternoon cutting down a huge pine tree in the yard, and we were just hanging out when his friend Jim came over for a visit. Jim was commenting to my father about how impossible it was going to be to get the giant tree stump out of the yard. Me, being a wiseass twelve-year-old boy, blurted out, "I could dig that out myself."

Jim laughed while replying, "Yeah, maybe in a month or two!"

Now my pride was on the line, and wanting to show him that I meant business, my response was, "I could do it in two days, and be finished by the end of the weekend."

Jim laughed and said "Yeah right, I'd bet a hundred dollars you can't do that!"

Having money from working my paper route, I called him out on the bet and asked him to shake on it. Jim looked at the three-foot-wide tree stump, and then looked at my father. Laughing, he commented, "I can't take money on a bet from a twelve-year-old boy."

My father responded, "Go ahead, and take his money if you think you can win the bet. He needs to know words mean something, and that a bet is serious. However, be careful Jim. It might not be a sure thing like you think."

Jim thought for a second, and then said, "I will take that bet, on one condition. No power tools or chainsaws. Only hand tools can be used."

"You're on!" was my reply, and we shook on it.

Now, Jim being a fullgrown man knew the level of hard work and hours that it would take to dig this giant stump out of the ground with just hand tools. Feeling confident after setting the terms, he chuckled a little and said, "I will stop by after work on Monday to pick up my hundred dollars."

All excited, I immediately ran off to the tool shed and grabbed a shovel and a pickaxe. Then I got right to work digging around the stump. At first, there was some good progress being made until I hit the roots. These were some serious obstacles! Some of the roots were six to eight inches thick, and it was now dark out. Not being able to see very well, I decided to go inside and get an early start on Saturday morning. Of course, to my complete surprise, when I got up the next morning, it was raining out! I mean, what twelve-year-old boy checks the weather for the weekend?

Now I had yet another obstacle to deal with. Luckily, having been brought up with my father's work ethic and having worked in the rain many times before, I had the mindset to just suck it up and keep going. Not to mention, a hundred dollars was like three months of my paper route money! Being out there all day in the rain, only stopping to eat and drink, made my hands all soft and pruned, causing blisters to form. My body was aching and sore from swinging the ax as I chopped at the thick roots, but I was determined to keep going straight through until dark again.

Sunday morning arrived, and I was totally dog tired getting out of bed. My limbs felt so heavy that it seemed as if I woke up on another planet with five times the Earth's gravity! Still, it was time to get back at it--and fortunately, the sun was out. At this point, my confidence was still pretty high, because progress had been made all the way around the stump. However, the physical toll that the previous day's work had taken on my body began to set in after just a couple of hours. The gas was getting empty in my tank, but the promise of winning $100 plus bragging rights gave me some serious determination to keep on going.

Standing in a hole waist deep, I walked around the stump attempting to push on it in every direction. Even then it wouldn't budge, not even the slightest bit. After all my efforts, it was as if the stump was still cemented in the ground. It was time to dig *under* the stump, not just around it. This is where the final push was going to be, and little did I know how much pushing was going to be needed. At this point, I was still ignorant about a tree's tap root. Digging underneath, I encountered the mother of all roots! It was the huge tap root that ran straight down into the earth.

There was no way to use the ax that I had used to cut all the other roots. There wasn't the room to swing it sideways underneath the giant stump. At this point, a feeling of defeat started to enter my mind. Climbing out of the hole and sitting on the edge of it, I stared at this enormous stump. I began to reflect on how far I had come. While sitting there considering quitting on the whole attempt, I realized it would be just plain foolish to give up at this point, so I ran off to go get a small hand hatchet. Laying on my side, four feet down in the bottom of the hole, swinging the hatchet with one hand at a time at this hellish tap root, it began to very slowly be chipped away. Crawling around on my belly from side to side while chopping away, the stump began to move a little.

This was the inspiration I needed. Adrenaline began to kick in, and eventually I cut through and could rock the stump in the hole. It was finally loose, but there was no way of getting it out of the hole because it was so damn heavy. Just rocking it an inch or two took everything I had. It was now late Sunday afternoon. I ran into the house to go tell my dad the stump was finally loose. "How is it going?" he asked, while smiling at me as a loving father does.

"Great, it's finally loose, but I can't get it out of the hole." I responded.

Following me out to the hole and inspecting my work to see if the stump was actually loose, he said, "I'm proud of you, but there is no way to get that huge stump out of that hole by hand. It's way too heavy for anybody to move. You go grab the chains and I'll go get the truck." After some twenty plus hours of working by hand and in the rain, the stump was finally pulled out of that hole on Sunday evening. Mission accomplished!

Monday came around and Jim showed up all confident to get his money, but the stump was out of the hole. Jim was shocked! He looked at my father asking, "Guy you must have helped him. There's no way Danny did this all by himself, and it even rained all day Saturday!"

Having a very proud dad moment, my father responded, "He worked completely by himself, and all day Saturday in the rain, too! All I did was pull it out of the hole with my truck after it was loose. Time to pay him the hundred dollars."

Work ethic is so important to accomplishing our goals. When we have a strong work ethic, we can accomplish things that other people view as impossible. If we are willing to put in the hard work that it takes to accomplish the things others think can't be done, we will get results that others think can't be achieved. This is what happened with Jim. He didn't think a twelve-year-old boy could work that long and hard to get that big stump out. Well, he was wrong, and it's time for you to do the same thing, and start proving the doubters in the world wrong. Be willing to go the extra mile and work hard, and don't let your own doubt get in the way, either.

Believe in yourself, and believe in the work you are doing, because this is the only way you will make your goals happen.

Reflect on your own life, and think of your own influences and the growth that you've had. No matter what age you were when the accomplishment was achieved or obstacle overcome, you will find some common themes. Who influenced you? How much effort did you put in? How did you grow through the experience? Reflect on these things in your own life, and use those lessons. We often forget the lessons we have already learned in life, and forget to apply the same concepts again in the present. Everybody does this at times, so we are not alone. The more you expand your mindset and look back at the influences you had and used, the more you will be able to look forward and reapply these lessons now in the present.

Also, look back at your life to remember something you worked really hard at and accomplished. Think of the motivation you had, and the discipline you used to keep going after it. Apply that same mindset to your next goal, or any obstacle that is in your path. You will amaze yourself and the ones around you with the things you can achieve.

I could not discuss my life's experiences of growth with you if I did not also share the things that I have learned from another one of my greatest influences: the study of martial arts. Everyone respects the hard work and discipline of martial arts, but another huge part of this is mindset. Studying martial arts is not for everyone, but there are lessons that can come from the arts which can be applied to everyone's life, including your own. These lessons relate to having proper focus, understanding what is important in life, and learning how to live one's life with a strong mindset.

When I was twelve-years-old, I attended a local town fair where there was a live martial arts demonstration for everyone's entertainment. I was captivated watching martial artists perform skills like breaking boards and even bricks with a bare hand! Before the presentation was all said and done, I was hooked. I knew I wanted to learn to become a martial artist. I convinced my parents to start classes the very next month. I was able to study multiple styles of karate to include Taekwondo, Kempo, and USA Goju. My karate school intensely focused on the ability to adapt to situations in life through a "hard-soft style." The principle of hard-soft is simply that sometimes you need to be hard as a rock in life, while other times you need to be soft and as fluid as water. At the end of each class we would focus our minds, meditate on these concepts, and recite a Dragon Warrior Code.

Throughout my study in martial arts, mindset was key. Helping me along the way was this Dragon Warrior Code that I memorized as a teenager, which I will share with you here:

Dragon Warrior Code

I am what I am, because I choose to be.

I am a dragon by choice, and subject to its loss.

My family, instructors, and my classmates are my heart and my mind.

Even though we may disagree with each other, we still strive to be one.

Forgetting all categories, and letting energy that wishes to exist, exist.

As a dragon I must go forth to seek the Tao in the void, understanding

myself, and finding peace within.

Learning this code helped me as a teenager to understand life better, and focus on what is important. Use this code, make your own, find another one, or construct something else meaningful to live by. Statements like these give us a sense of identity, purpose, and focus, and they can help guide you through life. These codes can become an amazing asset for us, so go find your own code to live by and use it. You will benefit more than you realize from having one.

Start with the first line of The Dragon Warrior Code, "I am what I am, because I choose to be." I have always found this line to be so empowering, and it can be for you as well. The first line gives us confidence in understanding that we are in control, and we can choose to be what we want to be in life. We get to focus our time and energy where we want. We can *choose* to be a positive force or a negative force.

As we continue to the second line, we realize that we are responsible for our choices and have to deal with the repercussions of the choices we make in life. When you replace *dragon* with whatever it is that you are, or want to be, you will understand that you are subjected to the results of your decision. If you choose to be a soldier who jumps out of perfectly good airplanes, then don't be surprised when you have back and knee problems. If you choose to be a server and carry heavy trays, don't be surprised if you get shoulder or wrist pain. You get the point, so now apply it to your own life, understand that you will have things to deal with based upon your choices, and then prepare your mind and body for them. Get your mindset right!

The third through fifth lines are great for understanding what is important in one's life, and how to deal with relationships. Let's dive into this a little more with, "My family, instructors, and classmates are my heart and my mind." Family, in general, is pretty obvious, but don't forget to include people who are as close to your heart as family. Instructors may seem unimportant because you may not have martial art instructors; however, this should not be overlooked.

Instructors are interchangeable with teachers or mentors. Think about how important a mentor was, or still is to you in life's journey. They are a huge influence, and a giant part of who you are today. A great teacher or mentor undoubtedly has helped you grow in many different ways. They are a part of your heart, always there lingering somewhere in your mind. I still hear the voices of my mentors giving me advice, as I am sure you do if you are listening. Don't forget to listen to them, because their words are priceless!

As far as classmates, I believe you are probably catching on by now. Classmates don't actually have to be classmates! They can be your peers, teammates, or even coworkers. These are the people that are walking the same path you are. Appreciate them, help them, and they will help you.

They, too, should be a part of your heart and your mind. Be very conscious of the people in your life, and you will be rewarded.

Next, we come to the part of acceptance. Now that you have realized the people in your life that are your heart and your mind, you will also realize that they don't always agree, or see eye to eye with you. This will always happen in life, so don't get hung up on it. Learn to let go. Learn acceptance. Furthermore, remember that even though you may disagree with each other, you still strive to be *one* . You will continue to go on working together to achieve goals and do something positive. For example, think of a loved one that you have had a disagreement with. You may have been very upset with them, but you still love them. You really do want the very best for them. We want to get beyond these differences, move on to what is really important, get back together, and be one with our goals.

A prime example of this is when I was deployed overseas with my teammate, Abel. He was the senior weapons sergeant on our team. Once, when I went to man my 50-caliber machine gun in the turret of my gun truck, I saw there was a new illumination system put on it. I did a basic functions check, and we rolled out of the Firebase. While out on patrol, I realized that the illumination system was limiting the mobility of the weapon, not allowing me total freedom of movement. I was not happy about this, and made sure I made Abel aware. As a typical type-A personality, I was calling him out and giving him a piece of my mind. He responded by giving me a piece of his mind, also, on how I should have done a better job inspecting my weapons system.

This went back and forth, and verbally escalated a lot. This can easily happen down range with the stress of being outside the wire in a combat zone. It escalated to the point where our Team Sergeant had to step in and tell us to knock it off, and that we would deal with it when we got back to base. Later that day, once we were back inside the wire, he called a meeting with Abel and me to straighten things out. When he arrived at the meeting, our Team Sergeant was ready to discipline us in order to work through and resolve our argument.

Instead, he was shocked to find that both Abel and I were calm, collective, and not mad. We had already worked things out before he even showed up for the meeting, and we had both taken ownership of what went down. We were one, and accepted each other's point of view. The fact that we had already resolved things on our own left our Team Sergeant pleasantly surprised, saying, "Well, that was easy to resolve." Even though we disagreed with each other on why things happened the way they did, we knew we were *one,* and the same with our goals.

Even more powerful is the line, "Forgetting all categories, and letting energy that wishes to exist, exist." Forgetting all categories is liberating yourself from stereotypes, biases, and the prejudices you have. It's simple and easy to say, but to truly do so is another thing. It takes true awareness and a certain mindset to accomplish. This couldn't be emphasized enough to help reduce your stress levels. This line is incredibly powerful and full of meaning. If you can learn to apply it in your life, you will begin to obtain a level of letting go that very few people will ever reach. This notion can release huge mental burdens and frees your mind from unnecessary stress. Many people think they are able to do this but are only fooling themselves, because they don't even realize they are doing it in the first place. This is a primal protective instinct that we all have, and we need to have real growth as individuals to get to a mindset where we can truly forget all categories.

The second half of this line involves letting go. Accept that you can't control everything around you. There will always be things or energy in life that you can't control. Let it go! Do not focus on it! Let it exist out there, and don't let it work its way inside of you and your mind. You can and should be aware of the things you can't control, but when something like that arises in your life, let it exist and don't fight it. This line of the Dragon Warrior Code always reminds me of some other very powerful words of wisdom: The Serenity Prayer, written by the American theologian Reinhold Niebuhr, which reads:

God, grant me the serenity to accept the things I cannot change,
Courage to change the things I can,
And wisdom to know the difference.

There are other versions of The Serenity Prayer out there, but you get the idea. Your acceptance of the energy which exists around you will give you peace of mind, and free up your strength to focus on the things you need to. This mindset is possible, and can be yours if you choose.

The final line in the Dragon Warrior Code is, "As a dragon I must go forth to seek the Tao in the void, understanding myself, and finding peace within." This summarizes what your overarching life goals should be, so let's break it down. "A dragon" in this line can be replaced with a father, mother, soldier, teacher, etc. Whatever you are, or whoever you choose to be, can be inserted there. To "go forth and seek the Tao in the void," simply just means to find your way in this existence or world. We all want to find our way, and by following the previous lines in the Dragon Warrior Code, you will be able to do so. You will also understand yourself, and who you truly are. When you put all of these lines together, and into action, you will obtain peace within.

The US Army Special Forces has its own prayer which is extremely meaningful and powerful. It traces its roots back to the birth of the United States, and the nation's oath of, "In God We Trust." The Prayer is very humbling as it is rooted in serving our fellow man, protecting their freedom, and not conquering them. Just like the US Army's Special Forces motto is "De Oppresso Liber," interpreted as "To liberate from oppression," or also commonly referred as "To Free the Oppressed," the prayer resonates this same message and more.

The Special Forces Prayer

Almighty God, who art the Author of liberty and the Champion of the oppressed, hear our prayer.

We the men of Special Forces, acknowledge our dependence upon Thee in the preservation of human freedom.

Go with us as we seek to defend the defenseless and to free the enslaved.

May we ever remember that our nation, whose oath "In God We Trust" expects that we shall acquaint ourselves with honor, that we may never bring shame upon our faith, our families, or our fellow men.

Grant us wisdom from Thy mind, courage from Thine heart, and protection by Thine hand.

It is for Thee that we do battle, and to Thee belongs the victor's crown.

For Thine is the kingdom, and the power and Glory forever,
AMEN!

Even if a Green Beret is not a religious soldier, the message, influence, and power of this prayer still reaches deep down into the soul of the Special Forces warrior. Defending the defenseless, and freeing the enslaved is in the blood of every honorable Green Beret.

While on the topic of influences in one's life and personal growth, it is impossible not to speak also about God. As someone who took an oath under God, sworn to protect the United States Constitution, I believe in the freedom of religion. I also believe we each have our own personal relationship with God. I know God has influenced my life spiritually while allowing me to grow as a person. Everyone has this same opportunity to benefit from God's love and guidance if we open ourselves up to it. God has given me peace in times of war and comfort in times of sorrow. God is my ultimate commander and my final judge. I will continue to pray that I am able to successfully carry out God's mission with love, honor, and dignity.

In this book, I have presented you with a philosophy in which having *The Asset Mindset* is an understanding that no one influences your life more than you do, positively or negatively, and you are your greatest asset. This does not by any means take away from God or God's influence in our lives, however. *The Asset Mindset* way of thinking only reflects an individual's free will to make choices in their life. The book is all about your choices, your actions in life, and where you want them to take you. It completely reflects on your own personal state of mind and faith. If your *Asset Mindset* chooses to take you down the path closer to God and connect with Him, then God bless you! If you have another way of thinking, then bless you, too! Either way, *The Asset Mindset* is yours to take ownership of and do with as you may. I wish nothing but love, success, positivity, and the very best in life for everyone who reads this book.

Chapter 5

Learning to Win

"Hey, look at that guy over there. He is ginormous and crazy scary! I sure would hate to have to fight him," said the martial artist standing next to me at the karate competition.

He was right! This guy had six inches plus on every other martial artist in the room. He stared down at everyone else like he was going to crush us all; he reminded me of Mr. T playing Clubber Lang in the Rocky movie. Nobody wanted to fight this guy, including myself! He was big, bad, and completely intimidating.

We didn't have a say in it, though. The referee took everyone's name cards, shuffled them up, and proceeded to start to pair us off to fill in the tournament fight brackets. Of course, it was just my luck that for my very first fight, I was paired with none other than Mr. "I'll crush you!" Beginning to feel lots of fear and doubt, the hair on the back of my neck stood up. I was completely intimidated.

Just then, something happened inside. My mindset changed. To be quite blunt, I got the "F@#K it" attitude. I told myself that I may lose, but I was going to give it my all. No matter what, he was going to get the best I had, even if I was going to get my ass kicked. My mindset had changed in an instant from being afraid to lose, to "I don't even care if I lose." "I am going to fight my ass off," I told myself, "and I'm going to show him what I am made of." When the referee yelled, "Fight!" I flipped the switch to *game on!* I hit him, and he hit me hard. It was an incredible fight that went back and forth, but everyone was stunned when I managed to pull off the win!

This win was a giant leap for me mentally, and it created so much growth in me as a maturing teenager. It was a fundamental experience in helping to facilitate my development of *The Asset Mindset*. There is so much that can be taken away from this story. Fear was overcome by courage, and the mindset to put everything into the fight. In doing so, the focus was no longer on fear and doubt. The focus was now on giving 100% and accepting whatever fate laid ahead. This mindset allowed me to achieve victory in the end. Not only that, but my level of confidence rose through the roof. Being victorious over "Mr. I'll crush you" showed me that everyone else there could also be defeated. That is exactly what happened, too. I did not lose a single fight through the entire karate tournament. After winning 1st place, this positivity bled over into the Kata competition (Forms competition). This is where competitors demonstrated their martial art skills through a series of movements in front of judges, where I also won 1st place.

At the age of 14, I ended up becoming a National Karate Champion in fighting and forms, and walked away with two 6-foot tall trophies. The lesson learned was, we can overcome our fear with the proper mindset. Our confidence, giving 100% effort, and the belief that we can accomplish any goal are huge factors in achieving success! Believing is a huge key!!! Ever hear of the placebo effect? It is real, and it has been scientifically proven again and again. Remember these key lessons that fear can be overcome, and believing in yourself can be incredibly powerful, even more than we realize. Apply these lessons to your own mindset during your life. You can obtain success and be victorious in your goals.

1991 Newspaper Article after winning two National
Karate Championships

Now, don't get me wrong; blindly believing in something without actually putting in the work does not do much good. Don't be surprised by the results you do not get when you haven't put in the time and effort to obtain them. If we want to win, we must show up. Yes, mindset and belief helped win the tournament, but hours of hard work and motivation were the foundation for the victory. As many Green Berets say, "the battle is won well before it even takes place." Now, really think about that and digest it for a bit. The hours of training, exercising, studying, shooting, and practice is what will lead to victory. Just like with any sports team that wins a championship, Green Berets also have to put the work in. The team that wins it all just didn't magically arrive in the championship game and become victorious. They put in hours, days, and weeks of effort to get to their victory. This applies to success across the board, whether you are a musician, police officer, teacher, nurse, chef, or in any career. To achieve success, we have to have the proper mindset that we can do it, and then put in the work continuously over time until we achieve our goal. Do not be afraid to fail at something. Be afraid of what could be lost if we don't even try. Never quit!

Speaking about effort and how work really matters, let's discuss my fellow Green Beret, Brian. I had the great honor of serving with him for most of my military career, starting before we both became Green Berets in Special Forces serving on the same A-Team. This man worked! Let me explain. He always was trying to better himself, and he was truly a guy who never took a day off. He was a beast in the gym, and even affectionately had the name "Meat" bestowed upon him because of it. He was 280 pounds of muscle when we were on the same ODA. On the outside, some might have thought he was just some dumb guy who spent hours and hours pointlessly in the gym banging weights around. Little would they know just how meticulous he was about his work ethic. He studied nutrition, how the human body worked, and planned everything he did with a purpose. By far the best workout partner I ever had, he was and still is an incredible asset to have in my life. I am forever grateful to him.

Going back to having an *Asset Mindset* and working your plan, Brian knew that strength was only one attribute of fitness. Brian always had an agenda, and stuck to it. His sincere effort and hard work allowed him to be a winner and achieve elite levels of fitness. He worked on everything, and for this reason, he wasn't just strong--he was fast. I recall a Green Beret officer one time calling him out, saying, "Yeah, you may be big and strong, but you must be slow." This officer was a runner, and took great pride in the fact that running was a great strength of his.

Brian, hearing this, and knowing how hard he had worked on complete total fitness responded with the challenge, "I bet I could beat you in a 50-meter sprint."

The officer laughed because he was a very lean, fast, and strong runner, saying, "I'll take that bet!" The officer thought he had this race in the bag; how would this 280-pound man be able to get all that weight moving faster than him? The challenge was on. They lined up, and someone shouted "Go!" The race started. Brian was really big and heavy, but so is a cannon ball, and they move awfully fast! Brian exploded off the start like he was that cannon ball, and crossed the finish line first. He had won the race. The Green Beret officer who was a lean mean running machine, and very fast himself, was in complete disbelief. He had lost, and asked, "How do you move that fast for being such a big guy?"

Brian responded, "I work on my fast twitch muscles, so I can move fast when I need to." This officer gave him lots of respect for winning the race, and from that point forward in his career. Over time, the respect continued to grow. It even developed into a sincere friendship between these two men.

This relates back to our subject of winning, and how we win at something. It takes hard work, dedication, education, and the motivation to do it all. Yes, that race only took a few seconds for Brian to win it, but he believed in himself because he knew how hard he had worked in the past. Not only did he educate himself to have the knowledge on what to do, but he also understood that to move fast, he had to work on fast twitch muscles. That's exactly what he did; he worked on everything. Brian was methodical about his fitness and his goals, which allowed him to be a winner. He still practices this very mindset today, and you can do the same. We can all get educated on what we want to accomplish, and learn how to be a winner. Take the time, have the motivation, and put in the effort. You will undoubtedly get positive results. Start setting yourself up to win today.

If you asked Brian today what you can do to be successful, he would most likely respond, "Just show up." He is so right! Most people want things, but they don't show up to make them happen. How many people want to be in better shape, but don't show up at the gym? How many people want an incredible career, but don't show up at the school to get the skills and degree they need? How many people want to achieve a goal, but don't show up to work on it? This showing up is the beginning of the process to make your goals become a reality, yet it's the hardest part for so many people to do.

If we want to win, we must *show up*. We need to put the time in, and there is no way around it. Everyone who is successful or has achieved greatness in any way had to show up first. Without showing up you can't be a doctor, lawyer, rock star, Special Forces, famous actor, teacher, or anything else for that matter. Start showing up in your life, and you will start achieving real results leading towards your success.

Brian and me while deployed

When we put all of the pieces together, we will learn how to win. We will realize that we need to get serious and show up in our own lives. We show up in life by getting educated, attacking it, and giving it our 100% effort to win. These things will lead us in the right direction to achieve our success. Believing in yourself is a magnificent and powerful tool you must utilize to help you achieve your goals. So, start believing in yourself now. We cannot let doubt or fear get in the way, or stop us from succeeding. Remember, fear is always an opportunity to be brave. Have courage, and grow. Once you understand these facts, you will begin to develop *The Asset Mindset* in yourself. This developing mindset is more powerful than we could ever imagine! When applied effectively, your mindset is the key factor for winning at life. You can and will learn how to win and succeed with *The Asset Mindset!*

Chapter 6

Creating Transformations in Life:
Citizen to Special Forces

Tired, half asleep, and stumbling down the stairs from my bedroom to eat breakfast, I turned on the TV to entertain myself. It was just like any other normal day. This day however, was very different and it was the day that a spark ignited inside me which changed my life forever. The spark would continue to grow until it engulfed my spirit, taking me down a path that 24 hours earlier I never would have imagined.

This was the morning of September 11, 2001. While sitting in front of the TV, I was seeing one of the World Trade Center towers engulfed in flames. To my shock and horror, I watched live on TV as another plane flew directly into the second tower. Along with the rest of the world who was watching, I gasped, and my heart ached witnessing the horribly tragic loss of life that I knew was taking place. I stayed glued to the TV for hours until my mind needed an escape to process the whole event.

Going out behind my family's home and sitting by the river to connect with nature, I tried to wrap my head around what was going on with the world. While sitting there, it was obvious that something inside had dramatically shifted. Somehow, I knew that the day's events were going to make a change in my own life path, as well. Like most people, when not knowing what to do, I found my mind wandering. Do I drive to New York City? Do I donate money? I was unsure of what to do, but continued to focus on the subject, looking inside myself for the answers. Of course, I was still glued to the TV and news for hours each day after the horrific attack.

Those who were close to me and knew me well could see something was happening. Changes were occurring inside me. Fast forward a little in time to when the U.S. military troops were being deployed to fight this extreme terrorism threatening the United States and the rest of the world. There was a huge national and patriotic movement back at home to support the troops. American flags and yellow ribbons were popping up everywhere. I witnessed soldiers on the news saying goodbye to their loved ones, hugging their children for possibly the very last time. This stoked a burning fire inside my spirit even more. I felt a huge connection with them, and a desire to support the troops; but in what way or how?

This is when it hit me. The best way to support the troops was to become one of them, and be with them by their side supporting their efforts. My decision was to become a soldier. Knowing what to do was no longer the problem. After focusing on and listening to my inner guidance, the decision had been made. The problem now was how to become a soldier, and where to go join.

It was time to get educated, do the research, and put the effort in so that the desired outcome could be accomplished. When we want to achieve something, we need to put in the effort to figure out how to make it happen. This resulted in reading many books on the different military branches and military schools, as well as talking with recruiters. The result ended up being an 18X contract with the US Army. The 18 is the designator for the Special Forces, and the "X" is there as an unknown, just like in mathematics. Just because an 18X contract was signed, it was completely unknown if someone would qualify to become a Special Forces soldier.

Almost immediately after signing the contract, I was told I wouldn't make it, but not to worry, because new orders would be given to me based on the needs of the Army. Luckily, *The Asset Mindset* lesson had already been learned: "Only you can tell yourself no, and to never quit!" Thanks again, Dad. My mindset was: I am going to do this, or die trying. The negativity others expressed to me about not making it in Special Forces did not really bother me, because I knew everyone's life is a complete unknown with endless possibilities. I knew that I was my own greatest asset in achieving my goals, and this gave me the mentality that I needed to manifest the future I desired. Just as you will face unknown situations and infinite possibilities in your life, remember to get educated, put in real effort, and realize you are your greatest asset to make your future dreams a reality.

It was early morning and the sun was just coming up, glistening off the dew in the grass. We were standing in formation getting ready for our first physical training (PT) test as new recruits. It was a warm wet spring dawn, enticing the worms and nightcrawlers to come up to the surface of the earth to suck up some of the moisture. The Sergeant overseeing the PT test walked around the formation asking what we each were going to be doing in the Army. When questioning me and hearing the response of "Army Special Forces;" he smirked and said, "Oh, I doubt it. If you are really going to be in the Special Forces, then eat that big nightcrawler worm by your feet." Having *The Asset Mindset* that I was going to do whatever it takes to become Special Forces, I immediately snatched that big slimy nightcrawler right up off the ground in half a second, tossed it in my mouth, and began to chew. Now, the look of shock on the Sergeants face was priceless to me. While eating this worm, the Sergeant's whole demeanor changed as he said, "I wasn't really serious about ordering you to eat that nightcrawler."

"Well, I am serious about wanting to be a Special Forces Green Beret," I responded.

"You are crazy, and you might just make it as a Green Beret," he replied.

The point here is that if you decide you really want to do or accomplish something, you will need to do unexpected and possibly unpleasant things to show people you are really serious about your goals. On a quick side note, you don't have to be this crazy. But if you ever have to eat a big nightcrawler to prove a point, I highly recommend that you grab the worm at one end and squeeze all the dirt out of it first before putting it in your mouth. Let's just say, if you don't do this, it makes for an awful crunchy sound in your mouth as you chew. It's not very enjoyable, and you can trust me on that one!

The path to becoming a Green Beret was far from easy. Along the way, I learned another mindset lesson: embrace where you are in the process.

Doing this will empower you and get you through all sorts of difficulties. However, it is truly up to us whether we embrace where we are or not. The path to becoming Special Forces is a long, hard road, with lots of stress that comes in many different forms. A soldier needs to embrace these stressful challenges, wherever and whenever. The idea of embracing stress can be considered synonymous with acceptance. When it's cold, hot, or wet outside, there is not much one can do about it. Let it go, and accept the situation. This translates to the very common military saying of "Embrace the suck!" A great tool that is used by Special Forces Operators all around the world to help embrace the suck is to use humor. Operators love to laugh and smile in the very worst of times and conditions. It is a great coping mechanism.

Use humor to turn things around when bad or ugly situations arise in your life. An example of this type of humor is when it would rain on us during a patrol; we used to say that you weren't wet until that first drop of cold water rolled down into the crack of your butt. It became an announcement to the rest of the team when that happened. An operator would say, "Oh, it is official, I am wet now, because a drop just rolled down into my butt!" Of course, this would lift the mood, and bring smiles to the faces of everyone else on the team who was soaking wet, too. Sometimes, it feels like we have a monkey on our back and we just need to roll with it. There are lots of other examples that could be shared, but the point is: embrace where you are in life, and use humor to make uncomfortable times feel better. Trust me, it really works.

Oh, and sometimes, you might really have a monkey on your back!

The next lesson along the path was the major mindset of taking ownership of a problem or situation. Doing this can truly empower us, and get us through many difficulties and confrontations. We all want to get past our confrontations and through our difficult times as quickly as possible. Often, people try to avoid owning the problem, and come up with some excuse or a reason which doesn't help resolve anything. The quicker we own the problem, the quicker we can solve the problem. Learn this lesson, and start applying it to the situations in your life. If we have the mindset of owning your situation, it empowers us with the ability to change or fix it.

During my transition to becoming a Green Beret, I forgot just one pair of socks that were on my packing list. This was a huge no-no. We can't forget anything on our packing list. When this does happen to one of us, we have to pay the piper and suffer the consequences of not having the required equipment by taking a trip out to the Gig Pit. For those of you not familiar with what a Gig Pit is, it's a pit designed for sucking and physical punishment known as corrective training. Most of them also have a hose that sprays super cold water at you while you are doing the exercises. They can be full of water and nasty swamp like mud which smells like raw sewage, or a foul-smelling low tide. There are also those that are full of sand to make the physical training punishment even worse, because the sand gets into all our crevasses while we are rolling around doing our corrective training. Just think of a time when you were at the sandy beach and you got some sand in a place that wasn't comfortable. Most likely, you removed the sand as quickly as possible. But imagine if you weren't able to. Then imagine doing pushups, flutter kicks, and jumping around doing other exercises with all that sand in those places. Not pleasant, right? Well, in our Special Forces training pipeline, we were blessed with multiple types of Gig Pits just to make sure it was all covered.

Now that you have a Gig Pit understanding, let's get back to ownership and embracing the suck, along with why this missing pair of socks story is being mentioned. While receiving some corrective training in our muddy sewer reeking Gig Pit, the Green Beret in charge told us to "camo up" after doing some push ups in this disgusting pit. This meant to take the sewage-stinking, nauseating cold mud and put it on your face like you were wearing camo face paint. Well, as you can imagine, who likes rubbing mud on their face that smells like raw sewage? Guys were half-ass faking it. They would just put small dabs on their cheeks and forehead. Instead, I decided to own the punishment, and embraced the suck. Reaching deep down under the cold water into the bottom of the Gig Pit, I grabbed as much of the nasty mud as I could hold in my hands. Then, pulling that repulsive mud up out of the water, I began to smear it over every single square inch of my entire face. When the Green Beret in charge of the Gig Pit session witnessed this, he pointed at me and said, "Hey you, you're done! Go take a shower and get cleaned up." I gladly did that while breathing as little as possible on the way to the shower to avoid enjoying another minute of the horrid stench all over my face.

After the shower, I walked by the Gig Pit. There were still some soldiers in the pit doing their corrective training punishments, also commonly referred in the military to as "getting smoked." Those soldiers were still struggling with their mindset. They were negatively moaning and groaning about how much this sucked for them. They needed to learn the lesson of taking ownership of their punishment for their mistakes, as well as embracing the suck. They were stuck. Myself and other soldiers who had the right mindset were able to get past the miserable suck fest of the Gig Pit much quicker. This mindset should be applied to your everyday life.

When we encounter something that sucks or makes us miserable, we need to own it, embrace it, and attack it head on. This is the fastest way to get through difficulties in life. If we half-ass it, trying to avoid discomfort just like some of the soldiers did who didn't really want to "camo up," then we will get similar results. We will be stuck in that situational Gig Pit of life longer than necessary! You can avoid this by focusing on owning your problems and embracing them. You will get much better results. Trust me; you may surprise yourself at how fast things can change. I was surprised when the Green Beret instructor, also known as "Cadre," told me to get out of the pit and go take a shower.

"Hey Dumbass," and "Hey sh@#head," where just some of the things that soldiers would be called by Cadre or their fellow soldiers all the time. We had to have thick skin. Oh, and those were the nicer of the names that were used! If the others were shared, there was a good chance someone might be offended, even though they shouldn't be offended at all. People shouldn't let words or names bother them. They need thicker skin, and so do you. Don't let people who are trying to get us all frustrated with name calling succeed. Have thick skin in your life, because it will definitely be tested at some point. Have a mindset that you don't care about the names, or what people say. Know who you really are as an asset. Who cares what someone else says about you if you have *The Asset Mindset*? Attributes of being Special Forces include having thick skin, *The Asset Mindset*, and not letting the little things said to us determine who we are, or affect our self-image. Be strong and have thick skin, so you can focus your energy on more important things.

Now, for the most powerful lesson learned during the transformation from civilian to Special Forces soldier: have heart. Heart means more than talent. Putting your heart into something comes with the willingness to work hard and having a never give up attitude. This will take us further than we realize. The key to having heart in our lives is that we acquire it, and most of all, we implement it into our lives every day. Do not go through life knowing you should have your heart in it; go through life actually living with your heart in everything you do. Having your heart truly involved in your life goals will create more success than you could ever imagine. This heart is the backbone of every Special Forces Operator, and the backbone of having *The Asset Mindset.* The great news is you don't have to be Special Forces to acquire and implement the powerful lessons about heart in your life.

To demonstrate the power of heart, we will discuss some things that happened during my transformation into a Special Forces soldier. It's no secret that it is a grueling task to go through, and even tougher to actually accomplish. Everyone, no matter who we are, will be pushed to extremes, which is why most people don't make it. Yes, at the beginning everyone says they know it's going to take heart, and they say that they won't quit. At least, everyone I came across said these things. Of course, it can be easy to say you have the heart and won't quit, but doing it is not the same. This coincides with the old saying, "Actions speak louder than words." This is another life lesson which was repeated by my father countless times, and should be instilled in all children as they grow up. When we live through our actions, not just our words, we will be living with *The Asset Mindset.*

Here is what happened. It was another early morning with the sun rising. All Green Beret Cadre were getting in position to run the last day's event for this phase of the course. It was time to see if the soldiers wanting to become a Green Beret could pass the Special Forces standards of the Physical Training Test, consisting of push-ups, sit-ups, and a run. The weeks before this day were long, grueling, and took a toll on every soldier's body, including my own. A soldier next to me was in so much pain that it had been difficult for him to walk in our barracks earlier that morning. I asked him if he would be okay, and he said, "I'm Fine. I got this." When the test began, he blew through the sit-ups and push-ups; however, next was the two-mile run. This man was having pain earlier just walking. How was he going to run two miles? Believe it or not, he did it, and did it in something like 12 minutes and 30 seconds! He had the power of heart and never quit attitude, and he knew he was his own greatest asset. He passed that phase, and was awarded his certificate.

After the phase certificates were awarded, the soldier raised his hand and told the Green Beret Sergeant in charge that he needed to see the Doc at the medical facility. Later that night, while back at the barracks, the soldier was wearing black boot walking casts. When asked what was going on, he said, "They did X-rays on my feet and I have stress fractures in both of them!" He then explained that he and the Doc were quite sure the stress fractures were more than a week or two old. Even though he could hardly walk earlier that morning, he had just run two miles at Special Forces standards with two broken feet! This hit me like a ton of bricks! Realizing how much heart and determination this man had truly motivated me. This soldier had true heart, and was going to be a future Green Beret.

That's real heart, and real never quit attitude; not just some talk about it. He had focus and his mindset was powerful, which carried him through the pain and the seemingly impossible task in front of him. Why didn't he say anything sooner? He wasn't going to say anything until after the phase was completed, so that he wouldn't be medically dropped from the course. If he had gotten medically dropped during the phase, he would have been dropped from the Special Forces Qualification Course and received new orders taking him somewhere else in the regular Army. This soldier wasn't regular, and didn't have the desire to be regular. He wanted more, so he waited to be awarded his phase certificate, knowing that after receiving the certificate he would be allowed the time to heal before starting the next phase in the qualification course. This soldier healed up, graduated, and donned the Green Beret, all because of his heart and never quit attitude. It was a true honor to serve with him, call him my brother, and I can't wait for our paths to possibly cross again someday. The last time we saw each other was when I was coming into Afghanistan as he was heading out. The next time we see each other again, we will pick up right where we left off. Most likely, he will call me some wise-ass horse nickname, which is more than okay with me. I will give him a big hug in return because names don't bother me, thanks to having thick skin and *The Asset Mindset*.

Let's take a closer look at who makes it through the transformation into becoming a Special Forces soldier, and how it applies to *The Asset Mindset* philosophy. There were men who everyone assumed would make it and didn't, and others who were assumed to fail, who made it. This definitely was and wasn't a surprise going through the Special Forces training pipeline. Flashback to airborne school: there was a jumpmaster Black Hat, (Black Hat is what airborne instructors are known as) who was constantly all over the soldiers training to become airborne qualified paratroopers. This Black Hat would preach about how only six percent of the military is airborne qualified, and how every soldier in Airborne School had to step up, and be in that top six percent. He was what in the military world we refer to as a "tab protector," meaning he would constantly try to get people to quit, or get them kicked out of airborne school to protect the integrity of earning the Airborne Tab which is worn on the sleeve of our military uniform. Ironically, soldiers can wear the airborne tab on their sleeve without going to Airborne School, if they are assigned to an airborne unit. In this situation, he would be better referred to as an Airborne wing protector, because you can only wear the medal or pin of Airborne wings if you have graduated from Airborne school. Anyway, the point is that this Black Hat would be considered a hard ass, and acted as though he was one of the toughest, if not *the* toughest, soldier in the world.

Moving forward in time to the Special Forces Selection and Assessment Course; guess who was there with me? Mr. Badass Black Hat! Immediately, the impression was that he was going to crush it, be selected, and become a Green Beret. He scored a perfect 300 on his Physical Fitness test, and already looked the part of being a badass Green Beret. It's funny, though, how the selection course is designed to challenge soldiers, and break them down. Surprisingly (or unsurprisingly, depending on how you look at it), about two weeks into the selection process, this Mr. Badass Black Hat perfect 300 score, quit! I never saw it coming at the time, but hindsight is 20/20, as they say. It makes sense to me now, but at that moment, it was completely shocking.

What happened was that this soldier was used to being the superstar, and getting through stuff easily. He easily got a perfect 300 score, and he could easily impress soldiers at Airborne school and make them quit. But there is no easy way to get through the Special Forces Assessment and Selection Course. No matter how fit, strong, and prepared you think you are, you will be sucking at some point. You won't be eating or sleeping properly, and you will be physically exhausted, so you need to have heart along with the never quit attitude to get through it. Unfortunately for him, Mr. Badass Black Hat was not able to embrace the suck when things did not go easily his way. He lacked the heart and mindset of a Special Forces Green Beret, so when times were too difficult for him, he quit. People who persevere and keep pushing through the hard times will achieve things that others will not, even if the others have more natural ability and talent. Create your mindset so that you are the one who has the heart, and pushes through hard times to achieve greatness!

On the other end of the spectrum is this guy who was in formation with all the other soldiers or candidates to become a Green Beret, who looked like he just shouldn't be there. Let's refer to this soldier as Littleman. He just looked skinny, frail, and not strong enough to be a Green Beret. Littleman was small and maybe weighed somewhere around 145 pounds. There are some rucksacks in the military that weigh around that much! My heaviest rucksack came in at 112 pounds alone, and that was just the pack, not any body armor or weapons systems. Soldier Littleman was looking at practically carrying a complete other self with him, depending on the mission or task. I had the great honor of going through multiple phases with soldier Littleman and eventually serving in the same Special Forces company. In every single Phase of the course, he impressed me with his heart, never quit attitude, and his strong mindset.

Every phase of the Special Forces Qualification course has different Green Beret instructors. Every time there was a new set of instructors, they would look at Littleman and think that this guy didn't belong. They would push him so hard to try and get him to quit. They would load him up with heavy radios and batteries, or a 240B machine gun. They would smoke the heck out of him, and on and on. Looking back, I recall a time that Littleman's rucksack was so big it looked like the rucksack grew legs. It appeared to be walking itself around, because you couldn't really see the rest of his body. Everyone underestimated Littleman, but that never stopped him from being the type of soldier that he already knew he was. Littleman looked like he didn't belong with these soldiers striving to obtain the honor of wearing the coveted Green Beret. But the truth was he more than belonged. He had *The Asset Mindset* and was the warrior they were looking for.

Littleman taught us all a very important lesson that is key to *The Asset Mindset*: don't ever let anyone stop you from being the person you know you can be. One of the fondest and most vivid memories of Littleman, which still makes me smile to this day, was in a place we referred to as "Camp Slappy." When I served, this training was at the very end of our pipeline, and it was a detainee type training. We all needed to pass this before we could graduate and be awarded the Green Beret. While training in this camp, the Cadre were trying to embarrass and belittle him in front of all the other soldiers going through the training. Littleman was ordered to stand elevated in the middle of our camp and yell, "I am a warrior," repeatedly. I don't know for sure why the Cadre did this, but a good guess would be because Littleman was so lean and frail looking that they thought this would completely embarrass him mentally or possibly break him, getting him to quit. He looked as if he had been a real-world prisoner for months. As all the other Cadre before had learned, Littleman was not easy to break. Every time he was told to yell, "I am a warrior," he would scream it even louder, and then louder again, and again! Littleman's mindset and warrior spirit lifted not just him up, but everyone else in the camp to the point that the Cadre gave up and had him get down. Littleman had experienced a huge victory, or as we were trained to call them *small victories*.

Littleman was a determined powerhouse because of his mindset. He came mentally ready to be pushed hard from the very beginning of the course. He was used to being singled out, tested, and challenged. He owned who he was, he embraced it, and he knew he was his own greatest asset positively or negatively. Littleman always made a choice to be positive, and he proved doubting Cadre and some of his fellow soldiers wrong, time and time again. He had the "special something" the Special Forces were looking for. He has what we have been referring to as *The Asset Mindset*, knowing he controls his destiny more than anyone else ever could.

Littleman went off to work at a place called Delta, and I'm not talking about the airline. Littleman's mindset was the cream of the crop, and as such, he continued to rise during his military career. This is why he eventually ended up at the most elite of military units, known as Delta Force. It was a blessing, and a true honor to serve with him for a period of time during my Special Forces career.

Putting everything all together now, we can see that the successful people who were able to transition into being Special Forces soldiers had a common theme. They were not always the biggest or fastest. Nevertheless, they were the ones with the biggest heart, strongest never quit attitude, and the positive mindset. They knew they controlled their own destiny more than anyone else. They took ownership of their life and the path before them. They embraced the difficulties in order to overcome and get beyond any obstacles in their way. We must understand these attributes, begin to develop them in ourselves, and most importantly, apply them. You own your life: embrace it, choose the direction you want to go, start heading down that life path, and don't let anything prevent you from doing so! Every day we get a chance to change and be different. Our past is in the past, so let's leave it behind us. Get on with making the changes you desire, transforming your life, and creating your own future.

Recall our earlier discussion of having a creed? You should probably not be surprised by now to learn that the Green Berets also have a creed of our very own: the Special Forces Creed. Here it is:

The Special Forces Creed

I am an American Special Forces soldier. A professional! I will do all that my nation requires of me. I am a volunteer, knowing well the hazards of my profession.

I serve with the memory of those who have gone before me: Roger's Rangers, Francis Marion, Mosby's Rangers, the first Special Service Forces and Ranger Battalions of World War II, The Airborne Ranger Companies of Korea.

I pledge to uphold the honor and integrity of all I am - in all I do.
I am a professional soldier. I will teach and fight wherever my nation requires. I will strive always, to excel in every art and artifice of war.

I know that I will be called upon to perform tasks in isolation, far from familiar faces and voices, with the help and guidance of my God.

I will keep my mind and body clean, alert and strong, for this is my debt to those who depend upon me.

I will not fail those with whom I serve. I will not bring shame upon myself or the forces.

I will maintain myself, my arms, and my equipment in an immaculate state as befits a Special Forces soldier.

I will never surrender though I be the last. If I am taken, I pray that I may have the strength to spit upon my enemy.

My goal is to succeed in any mission - and live to succeed again.

I am a member of my nation's chosen soldiery. God grant that I may not be found wanting, that I will not fail this sacred trust.

"De Oppresso Liber"

(Latin for, "To liberate from oppression")

This creed is extremely intense at times, but so is life. We need to face life with the same intensity that it will hit us with, if not more. We can transform ourselves, and our lives with *The Asset Mindset*, even if we run into hazards along the way. Do not fail yourself, or allow yourself to fail in achieving your goals. Push forward every day and you *will* experience positive effects which will alter your life.

Chapter 7

Being on a Team and Effects of Peers

It was a freezing -17 degrees outside, without the wind chill factor. It was pitch black out in the dead of night, and we were trekking through knee deep snow. We needed to get to the side of a mountain to pull 24 hours' eyes on observation of a target prior to our mission, and it was critical that we have our hide site constructed and be inside prior to the sun coming up, so that we wouldn't be observed. The movement went according to plan, and setting up the hide site wasn't bad (though, things would soon change, and the extreme cold temperatures would soon get really rough).

While inside the hide site, we couldn't really move around to create body heat to stay warm, so the temperatures became life threatening. We had no way to create more body heat, so we had to share what little heat we had between each other. This is when we got *really* close as a team. We snuggled up to each other and held onto each other like we were back at home holding our wives. There was undeniably some Green Beret battle buddy spooning going on; we must have looked like a bunch of puppies, each squirming around trying to get the warmest spot so we wouldn't freeze to death.

Being on a team, the peers we have around us can literally be the key to our survival or success. It truly is a blessing to have served on an ODA (Operational Detachment Alpha) with such amazing men who would support me and push me to be better. What an honor to call these men my peers. Many times, there were feelings of astonishment as to how I got to even be surrounded by such high caliber men with strong powerful mindsets. They inspired me and made me a better person. Who are your peers, what are their attitudes, and what are their mindsets? Do they inspire you to be and do better? We are who we associate with. There is the old saying my loving grandmother would use: "Birds of a feather flock together." Look at your flock. Are they flying high, or falling down? Remember, positive people with the right mindset will lift us up, and make us better. People with a negative mindset will bring us down, and hold us back. Being a part of a positive mindset team, or group of peers, can help lead us to the success we want in life.

Positive attitudes are contagious, and so are negative attitudes. Take a hard look at the people in your life, the groups you are involved with, and who your peers are. This can be very eye opening, and possibly very painful at times. We may come to the realization that we need to change some of the groups we are associated with, and even worse, distance ourselves from some of our peers. This is never easy. But this move is necessary, and will have a positive impact on our lives, if we make wise decisions. As we look at the groups we associate with and who our peers are, we will also notice the ones that are more positive. This will allow us to choose to spend more time working on the relationships which will enhance our lives in a positive way. Who doesn't want their life to be more positive, right? We have already learned that we control our mindset. We can also control where we spend our time, and with whom. Remember, attitudes and mindsets are contagious, so seek positive ones who will lift your life up. They will help take you to where you want to go.

Communication is another key to success. When in a group, with your family, or with your peers, you need to be able to have real communication. You need to be able to genuinely share your thoughts and dreams with them, as well as be able to listen, and learn. Sounds familiar right? After all, who knows us better than our family, peers, and close friends? They are the ones who will be able to help give us the best advice, but *only* if they have a positive mindset, themselves. Whether we are dealing with friends or family, it is always in our best interest to ignore the advice of people who have a negative mindset--or avoid it entirely.

It is also important to recognize that not all good advice is necessarily easy to stomach. We need to have thick skin for handling constructive criticism, which is extremely important for personal growth. Do not be afraid to ask questions if you want to know something, or if you are looking for ways to improve yourself. Ask people you trust, admire, and look up to, "how can I improve?" or "what should I be doing?" These, and other types of questions, can help make our ability to communicate much more effective, and will stimulate our personal growth. Remember, having and using good communication skills is another key to our success.

Having a solid team, or group of peers around us, can and will have a resounding impact on our lives. They may actually even save your life if you are ever stuck out in the freezing cold and need someone to snuggle up close with to make it through the night. That is an extreme situation, of course, but there are so many other situations in life where our teammates or peers can come to our aid. Teams can be incredibly powerful, and effective. That's why all throughout Special Operations they have and build specialized teams. Whether it is an A-Team (ODA), a SEAL Team, or any other type of specialized team; they have been proven, time and time again throughout history. Having a strong team around us is an amazing asset. Our teams may help us, or we may help them in more ways than we can imagine. Looking back on your life, I am sure you can find examples of this. You already know having a solid team works, so keep using this concept and building upon it. This strengthening of our teams will have a positive impact on our lives.

Start building or developing your own *Asset Mindset* team, and start reaping the benefits. Of course, it doesn't have to be modeled exactly like an ODA or SEAL Team. Yet, it will benefit you greatly to understand the concepts behind building these teams, so you can effectively build yours. Starting off, every member of a Special Forces team has a primary function or specialty they bring to the table, such as medical skills, expertise in communication with radios, weapons knowledge, explosives expertise, etc. It is set up this way to allow the team to have different subject matter experts so that they can work together more effectively in order to reach their goal. Understanding this concept, you should now apply it to your life. On your way to your goals, where could you benefit from bringing on a subject matter expert to help advance your own personal missions? Do you need marketing expertise, computer expertise, legal expertise, or assistance along those lines? What are your goals, and what type of teammates or subject matter experts should you have? This will help you build your very own *Asset Mindset* team.

We can have teammates for life, or we can also have temporary teammates for a particular mission or goal. Let's look at life teammates first. Although they don't necessarily have to be, they are the ones that will hopefully be there with us for the lengthy road of life. They could be someone who teaches us about life in general or how to be a good friend, mother, father, co-worker, etc. These people will be great assets when we are dealing with hardships or the challenges life will be throwing at us, which we all know will continue to happen throughout our entire lives. Our life teammates will share life's wisdom, and are an amazing asset to have by our side in our journey. Find and seek out people that have a successful life, who are full of life wisdom and positive life energy. We will recognize these people when we see them because they have this amazing spirit and mindset. They are the people who make us smile and feel good about life. Recruiting people like this to be on our *Asset Mindset* teams cannot help but make us better, and more successful as people.

Temporary mission teammates are almost as important as life teammates. These are the people who will teach us particular skill sets, or bring certain skill sets to the table to help accomplish a particular goal we may have. For example, when we would look for explosives, we would have a K9 soldier assigned to us who was a dog handler. This K9 soldier, along with his dog, made a great pair and were such an amazing asset to our team. They were not always a part of our ODA, but, when needed, they made a huge impact on the results we could achieve on our missions. Another example of this type of teammate could be someone like a music teacher who taught you to play the guitar. You had a goal to learn to play the guitar, and they were an asset that was on your team who helped you get there. You want to be a cook? Then go find a master chef. What is a goal or task you want to accomplish now? What type of teammate or asset could help you get there? We need to develop our thinking and have a mindset like this. The first thing to realize is what type of help we need. Secondly, identify the teammates we want by our sides. Remember, all of your *Asset Mindset* teammates should be a blessing, not a burden. Otherwise, they are not an asset to help you reach your goals.

We should be able to have complete trust and confidence in our *Asset Mindset* teammates; otherwise, they are not really a great asset to have. These poor assets or potentially negative influences were covered earlier when we discussed which environments, people, and excuses to avoid. However, when we do have true *Asset Mindset* teammates, we will realize that they are some of our greatest blessings in life. We will be more than willing to go anywhere or do anything with or for them. For example, there was my teammate, Leroy, who I trusted on so many levels, including with my life. He was an amazing medic on my team, but was so much more.

My life literally was in his hands countless times. He was my main gun-truck-driver while out on missions while I would be busy manning the turret, pulling security, and even more so during instances when he would walk in front of me while approaching an objective target building. This may not sound like a big deal to many people, but it truly was, because of my main responsibility on the ODA when raiding an objective. Being the master breacher on our ODA, I would be carrying the explosive breaching charge to blow the door to enter the target objective. This meant my M4 weapon would not be in my hands at the ready. It would have to be slung on my side. In other words, I didn't have a gun in the fight approaching a target, yet I always had complete confidence in Leroy leading me to the door. That is the caliber of an *Asset Mindset* teammate we want in our lives. We should be able to have complete trust and faith in that teammate.

Me giving orders while Leroy keeps an Afghan
soldier alive.

Then there is the simple fact that a true *Asset Mindset* teammate will tell us how it is, just like my buddy Chaca. He is amazing; the full gambit of a Special Forces soldier. He is always there to lift morale with his crazy 80's jokes, or he can just as easily get serious and look us in the face, telling us how it is. I remember one time when he looked right at me after completing an after actions report, and said, "You can't say that." It was true; because my report was a little too harsh with words, to say the least. However, after providing me with that feedback, he also helped me square it away afterwards. He won't pull punches, and has been known to push some buttons, especially if you are the new guy on the team.

When it came to me leaving the team, Chaca gave me some of the most straightforward and honest advice I ever could have asked for. He told me that Army life was only a temporary part of my journey, and that I could only ride the Army train for so long before I would be kicked off it and forced to retire--or even worse, killed, like some of our fallen heroes. Additionally, he advised me to not feel down, because I had done my share and honorably volunteered to go off to war to fight for my country. Furthermore, he told me that although I would be dearly missed, getting out for the sake of your wife and family is honorable because they are lifelong commitments.

This is the type of caring and honesty we need in our teammates or peers. We need people around us that will be truthful, and tell us how it is. It's like the old saying, "A true friend stabs you in the front, not in the back;" in other words, they will tell us there is a booger hanging from our noses instead of letting us walk around with it. These honest perspectives brought to us from our *Asset Mindset* teammates or peers will be very invaluable in our life journeys.

We have discussed for some time now what the right *Asset Mindset* teammates can do for you. But what can you do for them? Our *Asset Mindset* teammates are great and wonderful assets who will lift us up in life. Conversely, did you notice that the best teammates provide something, and always bring some sort of benefit to the table? They are an asset, and will have a positive attitude. They have the type of mentality and desire to *help others around them*. This is who we need to become, as well! We need to be the best possible teammates we can be, and always be willing to give to others. Positivity works best when we pass it on. Think about it: the best teams have the best players who work really well together. Bring *The Asset Mindset* philosophy with you to share with your teammates or peers in life, whenever you get together, and the effecting results will be overwhelmingly positive.

The most amazing and wonderful thing happens when we are an asset to our peers. The more we give to our teammates, the more we will receive.

It sounds like a cliché, but it really is true. I could provide an endless list of examples of this principle at work in my own life, but here, we will just discuss one. My former Special Forces teammate Chase and his wife were having a baby in the near future, so to be as supportive as possible, I made a visit to his home, and gifted him and his wife with a card and a decent sum of money as a gift to help out with the baby. We had a wonderful visit that went on for hours.

Later on that day, while hanging out in Chase's garage doing what team guys do, I was bestowed an amazing gift. You see, he had replaced his rifle scope with a brand-new state of the art one, and he gifted me his old scope for my new rifle. This old scope was a very valuable and high-quality scope. He would never own anything that was not a high-quality rifle scope, because this guy wasn't just a sniper; he was also a Special Forces sniper instructor. He didn't own cheap rifle scopes. I didn't want to take it without giving him some form of payment, but he adamantly insisted that I just take it.

The purpose of my visit to his home was to go there to be a giver, in support of his growing family, and ironically, I left with an extremely valuable gift myself. It is a wonderful thing when we are on a team where everyone is paying it forward to each other. Again, positivity works best when we pass it on. Be the person with a strong positive mindset, and you will attract others who think the same way.

The fact is, the people we surround ourselves with, the friendships we make, and the teams we build will have an enormous impact on our lives. Really be honest with yourself on who your peers are. Do they elevate you to be better, or are they holding you back? We need to choose them wisely, and we need to project *The Asset Mindset*. We must identify people who are our positive assets, and be conscious of how we can be a positive asset in return to others in our lives. Don't limit yourself to just one "team" or "sport," so to speak. Be willing to push yourself to join other groups and all the teams you want to be on. Go after your dream teams, showing the people in these groups you belong and deserve to be there. The decisions we make about our teammates and peers are an asset to us and our lives, or a hindrance. Choose and act wisely, because your success depends on it!

In the middle surrounded by a great team of men.

There is another concept that is commonly used in the Special Operations community, referred to as the "Dead Test." I know that the concept may sound morbid to you if you're a civilian, but hear me out. This test is an assessment of how our death will affect our teammates and mission. The concept of the Dead Test relates to many situations or subjects, but is always based on the theme, "What happens if I die?" The Dead Test can and should be applied to our lives, as it relates to taking care of our *Asset Mindset* teammates, such as family and loved ones. When assessing life's situations, we need to take into account what would happen to those around us if we died. Would we leave the people around us lost and confused as to what to do? Would we leave them with a horrible mess to deal with?

If we have *The Asset Mindset*, and are a good asset to our families or teams, they should be set up for the best possible success in the future. Your family or team's mission should be able to continue to move forward in life as positively as possible upon your death. An ODA example would be making sure we shared any critical information, resources, or instructions with our team so they could continue the mission without us. It would be a horrible situation if we died on a mission and we were the only ones who knew where the exfiltration point was, right? The last thing an operator wants to do is leave his brothers hanging because of something he failed to plan for. It's not easy to think about dying, but it is something everyone must accept. It is going to happen sooner or later. Plan for death, so you can leave those you love who are left behind in the best possible situation. When we have *The Asset Mindset,* we will prepare and plan for the Dead Test.

What does the Dead Test mean to you, and how can you use it? It means, set your life up so your family, loved ones, and others around you will be in the best possible situation upon your passing. Do you have term life insurance (not whole life insurance) to provide for the ones you love? If not, go get it. Does your family know what your wishes are upon your passing? Make sure to talk to them. Do you have a will? If not, make one, or update the one you already have if necessary. Have you said all the things you need, or want to say to them? Communicate openly and honestly with them. This Dead Test is not fun, or easy to do. Nevertheless, if we really want to be the best asset we can be for the people around us, whom we really care about, then we need to think about the Dead Test. When we have *The Asset Mindset*, we will start thinking in this way and apply the so-called "Dead Test" to our life's circumstances.

No longer being on active duty on an ODA team, but still staying involved in the Special Operations community, I have made some observations about post team life and being a former action guy. One observation is that some former action Operators may have their mindset change in different ways. They don't focus on their mindset as consistently as they used to. Some let themselves go, both physically and mentally, because they feel their time of being a badass warrior is over. Others aren't involved at all with the Special Operations community anymore and move back to where they came from. This can be detrimental, because they can fall back in with old friends with bad habits and lose *The Asset Mindset,* which they established while in the military serving on a disciplined team. These men have free will and can do whatever they choose with their lives. It is their life to live the way they want to live it. However, these former action guys have lost some of the positive team influences which helped them become the successful elite soldiers they were while on active duty. Faithfully having *The Asset Mindset* means to continually work in the present to build a better future. Don't let a changing environment or situation change your mindset for the worst.

Please do not take me the wrong way; these men are still real heroes, and I am forever grateful for their service and sacrifices. I only mentioned this here in order to emphasize the power of influence and having positive people around us who will keep us motivated to push ourselves to be better. Even elite people from all backgrounds, when not surrounded by a positive group or team, can be subject to decline as a result of this dynamic. Who we surround ourselves with can be a positive influence, or negative influence in our lives. Always keep this in mind, because it is true for you and everyone else. No matter where someone might have been or what someone may have accomplished in the past, it takes a continuous effort to maintain positive influences and *The Asset Mindset*. The same applies to us and our life's success.

This is why *The Asset Mindset* should become a lifestyle, not something that is only applied in our lives temporally. The former action guys who are no longer in the military but still maintain *The Asset Mindset* will continue to grow and push themselves, no matter what. They will continue to surround themselves with a positive team of people. They realize that no matter what we have done in the past or where we are currently, we always need to keep pushing our lives in a positive direction. This is reflected in the old military saying, "You never stop improving your fighting position." In the same way, never stop improving in your life! Live with *The Asset Mindset* as a lifestyle.

On the subject of lifestyle, let me share another story of an amazing man. Romy Camargo is a former action guy who we were blessed to have in my Special Forces Group, and who I got to know personally during a military school we attended together. This soldier was someone people would call the complete package. He was first an enlisted soldier, became an Army Ranger, became a Special Forces Green Beret, and then became a Chief Warrant Officer in the Army Special Forces. He was always moving forward. But one day, he was tragically wounded in his cervical spine becoming paralyzed. Later sharing his story with his facebook followers, he wrote:

"I want to let everyone know what happened to me that changed my life forever. On September 16, 2008, while my team and I were conducting

combat operations in Afghanistan, my small task force came under an ambush. During the ambush I suffered a gunshot wound to the back of the neck, paralyzing me instantly. As the firefight ensued, my team was able to stabilize me and got me out of the area where I was then transported to several airfields in Afghanistan and then on to Germany. Once I was in Germany, I was then accompanied by my brother. After spending 11 hours in Germany, I was then transported to Walter Reed Army medical Center. While at Walter Reed, I underwent a nine-hour surgery to stabilize my neck. I was then transferred to James A. Haley VA Hospital in Tampa, Florida, where I began my rigorous physical therapy regime which included a strong respiratory program. I spent a total of 18 months at the VA. I decided to stay in Tampa since I was close to my family. I now own a beautiful house and continue to conduct physical therapy. I am currently looking at different things in order to improve my situation. I will definitely keep everyone informed on my progress."

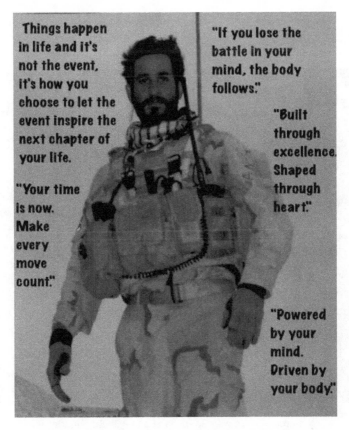

Things happen in life and it's not the event, it's how you choose to let the event inspire the next chapter of your life.

"Your time is now. Make every move count."

"If you lose the battle in your mind, the body follows."

"Built through excellence. Shaped through heart."

"Powered by your mind. Driven by your body."

Online post by Romy demonstrates he has *The Asset Mindset*

Romy has *The Asset Mindset* and has made it a lifestyle. He could have easily given up, focused on the negative, and spent the rest of his life being a victim, but he hasn't. He is absolutely amazing, still pushing forward, and is still changing the world to make it a better place. He continues to surround himself with positive people, and he has created another team to take things on and face life's new challenges. To inform you of his progress, Romy and his wonderful Gabriella have founded: Stay in Step Spinal Cord Injury Recovery Center (www.StayinStep.org) where Romy is the acting director. Please go check out Stay in Step, because it will definitely motivate you with stories of dedication, hard work, and commitment to improve people's lives. Romy was a leader in the Special Forces community, and still is a resilient leader to this very day by living a lifestyle consistent with *The Asset Mindset.*

Romy with his wife Gabriella at a Stay In Step fundraiser

The Asset Mindset tends to turn us into a natural leader for others to follow, whether we realize it or not. When we have a strong mind, we will take ownership of our life's direction and our life's purpose. People will naturally follow us when we are moving forward in such a way that we are not afraid to accomplish our objectives. My ODA Team Sergeant, Bob, also known as a team daddy, was responsible for our ODA in Afghanistan. He was this type of leader. He was a hard charger, and we all knew when Bob got fired up, there was no stopping him. If he wanted to go down a certain path or enter a certain compound, we followed. Due to his strong mindset as a leader, it was just natural for us to follow him anywhere.

Looking back now, one of my outrageous memories from our deployment was doing just that. Bob decided that we were going to enter and clear a compound in this large hostile village. There were a significant number of Green Berets on the mission that night who were tasked with securing this entire village, and it was so big that when we arrived at the last compound there were only three of us available to enter and clear it. This was an intense split-second decision, because it was only Bob, Brian, and myself who would be entering the completely unknown threat of that compound.

Having only three Special Forces Operators is not the ideal situation for conducting close quarters battle (CQB), but he made the decision three of us were going to do it. Brian and I proudly followed his lead and entered the compound with him. While inside, we cleared every room and took control of everyone inside, which if I recall properly was a total of eighteen people: five fighting age males, and 13 women and children. This was not a perfect situation for us, but with Bob's mindset and leadership, three Green Beret operators took complete control of the situation inside that compound. We were able to accomplish this task because of his effective leadership, belief in each other as solid teammates, and having the strong mindset that we were in control. Our mindset was one that we were going to make it happen no matter what we faced inside. Positive leaders such as Bob help create positive mindsets where you believe in yourself and each other.

When we have *The Asset Mindset,* people will follow us, gravitate to us, and they will take notice of us more. These observations will get us added attention we may or may not want. The fascinating thing is that positive people with similar mindsets will be drawn to us or want to be associated with us. Even though people with a negative mindset may say negative or hurtful things, remember to have thick skin. These negative mindsets will eventually want to distance themselves from us. It is quite fascinating that our positive mindsets threaten their negative belief systems so much that they want to stay away.

Remember, it is always possible for our positive *Asset Mindset* to help change other's negative mindsets around for the better. Don't get me wrong; this does not mean we will never have to deal with jerks in our lives again. It's just that now, when we do, we will have a strong *Asset Mindset* to handle them and push them aside, so they do not block the life path we are on. Doing this may also leave some additional space around us for other positive people to take notice and fill in any voids. Leaving us with the ability to create a strong *Asset Mindset* team from our peers. *The Asset Mindset* philosophy creates a place for us to be blessed by others and for us to bless individuals who are around us or drawn to us.

Chapter 8

How to Make Habits Become Assets

The choices we make and the actions we take are undoubtedly crucial to the positive or negative outcomes we experience in our lives. There needs to be motivation to make the right decisions. We need to really want it. We need to have a fire inside, and a serious heart in us to stay motivated. We can't exercise once and expect to be fit, or eat one salad and expect to have a healthy diet. We need to continually stay motivated in pursuit of our goals. This is not easy, but the more we do it, the easier it becomes. This repetition will create a habit resulting in a positive outcome for us. You are the creator of your life path, and your behavior is how you succeed or fail. Creating good behavior will develop positive habits, which bring about positive effects that we can include in our daily routines. These positive behaviors are a choice, and we need to make them habitual, which will undoubtedly lead to the successful life results we are looking for.

What are some of the best habits you can have in order to be successful? To start off, get up early. We all know the old Benjamin Franklin saying, "Early to bed, early to rise, makes a man healthy, wealthy, and wise." This was very true years ago, and is still completely valid today. In the Special Operations community, we may go to bed very early, around noon, to be up all the next night and through the next morning to catch the bad guy. It's kind of like the early bird gets the worm, only the early Special Forces Operator catches the bad guy!

This is not an exaggeration. I recall one time when we actually woke a bad guy up and dragged him out of his bed. We made it all the way into his room without him knowing! What a great success that mission was. Side note: if you ever get a chance to do anything like that, don't yell at the bad guy to "get on the floor" louder, and louder in English, when they don't speak it!

That's what the first guy in the room did after waking him up, and it didn't work out too well until I entered the room right after him and demanded in the bad guy's native language that he get on the floor. Luckily, I was just a few feet behind, as I was the third man who entered the room, so no one got shot. We were able to apprehend our target without incident. This made for a nice joke among the team later, that yelling louder in English doesn't help a bad guy understand you any better. As you can see from this example, getting up early can help you accomplish your goals--and proper communication helps, too!

In the midst of our busy lives, getting up early can give us the "me time" that everyone needs. We can use this time for exercise to help keep our greatest asset (ourselves) strong and healthy. We can use this time to plan our day and week, or reflect on our short- and long-term goals. This time can also be used to make progress on some projects we may be working on. Get up and get moving, because that's what people with *The Asset Mindset* do!

The next habit we will cover is the need to continually learn and educate yourself. If you have *The Asset Mindset,* you need to keep growing as a person, and never stop! A great habit used to accomplish this is to read daily. There have been countless studies about successful people and how a huge majority of them read daily. One such research study comes from Tom Corley, who found that 88% of his wealthy respondents said they read for 30 minutes or more each day, primarily focusing on self-improvement or education.[2]

On an ODA, Operators are continually training, going to new military schools, reading field manuals, or conducting cross training among themselves. In the Special Forces community, we continually strive to improve and get better, because we know that being just good is never good enough. There is always room for improvement. A perfect example of a team cross training event was doing IV medical training amongst ourselves. I remember sticking my teammate and not holding pressure down on the IV catheter when reaching for the IV line, only to have his blood come gushing out all over the place. Needless to say, I got teased after that, hearing, "Don't let Dan give you an IV, because he will help you bleed out!" This was another example of needing to have thick skin when trying to learn new things. Always take any criticism and turn it around to be constructive, not destructive. After conducting that IV training, I never made that mistake with an IV again. Continue to learn, practice things you know, educate yourself, and read, because these habits will all lead you down the path of personal growth.

Another must-do habit is to spend some time each day on focused thinking and reflection. Look at what you did or didn't do that day. Reflect on how you could have done things better, and what you did well. We would do this constantly in the Special Forces community. We called this reflection time an "After Actions Review" (AAR). This AAR habit is where we would "make our money," meaning that AARs paid off big dividends towards our improvement. You need to make this daily AAR habit pay off for you. A simple format which can be used for an AAR is to break it down into three sustains and three improvements, if you can.

Here's what that looks like. Each day, take time to reflect on three good things you need to keep doing, and three things that did not go so well, where you have room for improvement. If we do this every day, we will be pleasantly surprised at the progress we can make. Definitely feel free to conduct an AAR at any time after a task or event you may be involved with. Include others in this AAR process whenever you can, as well. Your Asset Mindset teammates or peers could have some very valuable observations and input. Thinking and reflecting is a great habit and tool for improving our lives. Do an AAR as often as you can, whenever you can.

The following habit was briefly mentioned before, but definitely needs to be addressed again with more emphasis. We need to get in the habit of exercising regularly, and make it a priority. It is such a huge priority in the military that it is the first thing conducted every day. Every morning starts off with a PT (Physical Training) session, unless there is a greater mission or task to be completed. Otherwise, every day starts off with exercise.

There are so many benefits to exercise that we can't even begin to discuss them all here. Just a few of the major benefits of exercise are clearing and sharpening the mind, burning off stress, and helping us feel more motivated. All of these results are supported by endless articles and scientific studies. Now, imagine being able to walk into a store where you could purchase an upgraded version of yourself that feels happier, has stronger muscles and bones, has more energy, is more resistant to chronic disease, feels less pain, *and has a better sex life!* Sold, right? Well, you can't walk into a store to buy that version of yourself, but you absolutely *can* walk into a gym and earn it! Truthfully, you don't need to walk into a gym; you just need to make sure you get quality routine exercise at home or outdoors. Make exercise a habit. Stay active and stay healthy.

Exercise is a critical aspect of having *The Asset Mindset* for many reasons. You need to be responsible and take care of you, because ultimately you are your greatest asset to having a successful and positive life. Furthermore, we need to *own* our fitness, because no one else can do it for us. By no means do we need to spend hours upon hours in a gym, but we do need to be proactive to get in better physical condition. Even twenty to thirty minutes a day can make a huge difference. Find or create an exercise routine that works for you. The key is to make time and prioritize exercise as part of your life. Always strive to get better and not lose any progress you have made once you have started. Exercise will definitely benefit us throughout our entire lives, so make it habitual!

Get in the habit of spending time with people who inspire you and make you want to be more successful in life. This habit is closely associated with the team topic and the people we spend our time with as referenced earlier. We need to be routinely around positive people whose productive habits rub off on us. Surround yourself with people who can be considered balloons and will lift you up, and stay away from people who are anchors who hold you down. Anchors attempt to sabotage you or others who try to achieve, or are attempting to achieve success. This can be based on many things like jealousy, envy, or other negative feelings. Remember, stay away from those crab mentality people! The point is we need to make it a habit to associate and spend our time with *balloon* people who inspire us and help us grow. They are the ones who enlighten us and raise us up in life. Make it a habit to surround yourself with a solid group of *Asset Mindset* teammates who support you.

Be in the habit of getting enough sleep or the right amount of sleep. Getting too much sleep can be just as bad for our success as getting too little. Having the proper amount of sleep is critical when it comes to mental function, perception abilities, and even our creative thinking. Everyone's sleep needs are a little different, but experts regularly suggest that 7-9 hours seem to be around the proper amount for most adults, based on what the National Sleep Foundation recommends. Sleep needs will vary based on age and activity levels, of course, but it is key to get the proper amount for both our minds and our health needs.

Trust me, lack of sleep will be detrimental to our minds, and it will do strange things to our perception. Being truly sleep deprived one time during a training mission was a real eye opener. We were in a patrol base for the night, and while covering my sectors of fire (or area of responsibility for security), I watched a bush turn into a person who was trying to sneak up on us. Tapping the soldier next to me to alert him somebody was out there, I then rescanned the forest. I subsequently watched it turn back into a normal bush again! It was the first time I had hallucinated due to lack of sleep. This is an extreme example of not getting the proper amount of sleep, but it shows just how important sleep really is. Oh, and don't you worry! There was lots of teasing about seeing a "Bush-man-bush" after that, too! Yet again, it was helpful to have thick skin.

Sleep helps the body recharge itself, so don't be afraid to take naps if your body needs it. If you ever meet a Special Forces Green Beret, ask him when was his last "GBNT." He will probably look at you with a smile, and say some smart-ass comment, or say he could use one right now. You see, "GBNT" stands for Green Beret Nap Time! Yes, it is a real thing, and not a joke. When we do operations and missions through all 24 hours of the day, we need to squeeze in some power naps. Green Berets and other Special Operations soldiers have this uncanny ability to sleep just about anywhere. When your body needs recharging, take a nap wherever or whenever you can. Get the sleep your body needs to stay healthy and alert.

A prime example of Green Beret nap time "GBNT"

Consider also looking into the habit of practicing meditation as a way to recharge and energize your body when tired. Meditation can also be used as a way to clear up mental blocks and past traumatic experiences. Many warriors from different cultures, from past to present times, have used different types of meditative techniques to increase their performance. Meditation can help relieve stress, relax our minds, and help create better focus. All of these attributes can help lead to achieving our goals. The Dragon Warrior Code, discussed earlier, was used as a meditation during my early years of martial arts training, which you may use as a starting point. There are also plenty of research studies and books to read on meditation. An easy read and one very user-friendly book is, "Stress Less, Accomplish More," authored by Emily Fletcher, who has spent some time working with Special Operators from the Navy SEALs. One of Emily's key quotes is, "We meditate to get good at life, not to get good at meditation." Meditation can recharge our bodies and give us energy, which in turn can improve our personal and professional lives if we make it a habit. Emily can teach you that meditation is not just for monks, and her book will show you how you can fit it into your own lifestyle. Meditation is a tool we can use to create the positive mindset and success we are looking for in our lives.

An additional habit we need to cultivate is to learn to be constructive with our time. Avoid bad habits that will waste your time. Get in the habit of appreciating the time that you have. The proper use of our time is crucial to reaching our goals. When we invest our time in doing something, we can never get that time back. It is lost forever. How many hours have we all wasted on bad habits, or on modern devices with games, social media, and watching television? We need to avoid time wasters that don't help us grow. Not wasting time seems like a no brainer, but time is commonly taken for granted.

It can be very difficult to change our behaviors so we can make the most of our time. Remain conscious that you and everyone around you only have a limited amount of time. We are all going to die at some point, and it is inevitable. The moment you truly embrace this is the moment when you will free your mind to understand that you should make the most of the time you have. To quote entrepreneur and author Robert Ringer, "I wish I could be the bearer of good tidings and tell you that you have unlimited time to stare at the ball and decide what you're going to do with it, but that's not reality. Like all games, the game of life must end, and the clock is ticking as you read this!"[3] Make it a habit to be positive and constructive with your time.

Use your time wisely, because it is a resource or asset that we cannot get more of. Time is like gas in our fuel tank, except for the fact that we start off with only one full tank, and we can never refill it. Not to mention, there is no fuel gauge on our time, so you never know when it will run out. For this reason, do NOT waste your time just idling in life! Use your time wisely to go somewhere you want to go. The best thing we can do to help with having the most time as possible is to transform the body into a fuel-efficient vehicle. Take good care of your body by eating healthy and exercising. Doing this will also make the journey more enjoyable along our way. Our time resources must be used wisely to reach our full potential and achieve our goals.

We should start to see losing time as one of our greatest risks. The more we become aware of how precious and valuable time is, the more we will invest our time wisely. In other words, if we fear losing or wasting our time being idle, it will force our minds to see time as the extremely valuable asset that it is. Nobody likes to waste their resources or assets. This concept of time will help create motivation within you. Thinking of time as a limited asset, which it ultimately is, will cause us to be more aware of how and where to invest our time. Start viewing losing your time as a giant risk, and you will become motivated to not waste this precious commodity anymore. This understanding of time will help you in establishing better time management skills, becoming more efficient in life, and in creating *The Asset Mindset* in your head.

All of the habits we have discussed here are each a key asset to creating and becoming successful in our lives. Putting these habits together will create behavior which will shape and change your future in a more positive manner. Always moving forward in a positive direction is extremely crucial for success. We must routinely behave in such a manner which allows us to obtain our life objectives. We must create positive habits and pursue our goals daily! We need to be relentlessly and consistently moving forward in the pursuit of our goals, both short-term and long-term. Yes, some days we will be more productive than others, and some days we need to relax and have fun enjoying life. It is a balance, and enjoying life should be one of our ultimate goals.

This doesn't mean that fun and relaxing days are not part of our plan to reach our goals. Moments of relaxation can add value, creativity, and help provide direction, along with allowing for us to build back up our energy storage. Embrace those days, and every day, take a big or small step in the right direction towards your goals. Find a healthy balance and enjoy life, while at the same time creating a mindset where you are still laser focused. Focus your mindset on your goals in such a way so not a single day goes by without you spending some time thinking about and pursuing them. It is so crucial that we pursue our dreams and goals daily, if we are serious about creating change in our lives and reaching our desired levels of success. We are now creating a lifestyle with behaviors and habits which are focused on building *The Asset Mindset*. We *can* be successful and achieve our dreams.

Chapter 9

Making Changes, and Planning Techniques

Stop making excuses in life, and start making changes. There are always excuses out there that can be used as a reason to not make a change. Don't use them. Take ownership of your life! When we own our lives and focus on training our minds to change in a positive way, we will definitely think and act more positively. This process allows us to actually *become* our positive thoughts. Becoming these positive thoughts can then lead us to create more positive lives. Simply put, our positive thoughts can become our positive reality.

Nobody is in the driver seat of your life more than you. Yes, we will all experience conflicts or resistance to change at times, just like sometimes it storms outside. Yet, no storm lasts forever, and although we may need to hold on tight during a storm, it will always pass. The sun will come out eventually. Challenges in our lives work the same way. The storms, or challenges, in our lives can actually benefit us just like the grass benefits from the rain. The grass needs the sun, but it also needs the storm's rain in order to grow, and so do we. We can mitigate the negative effects of a storm by having prepared ourselves mentally ahead of time, understanding the storm is temporary, and the storm is an opportunity for growth. Stop making excuses, or coming up with reasons why you can't make changes in your life. Start making the changes you desire now.

Our focus matters. Where we put and spend our energy matters. If we desire to be a better version of ourselves, we need to put our focus and energy into the process of making our vision a reality. Many years ago, while still in college, I shared the concept of being a page master while talking over some life issues with close friends. A page master is a concept based on the idea that the mind is like a book, and our thoughts are the pages. We have the power to turn to a different page or even a new chapter; we are always free to focus on the pages we want and enjoy most in our lives. Every mind works a little differently, but we are all the page master of our own story, or mind. We can keep reading the same negative pages over and over again in our heads, or we can choose to turn the page, allowing us to think about something more positive. Most people do this type of repetitive negative thinking subconsciously, which is why they will often get stuck in an undesirable mindset. Countless people don't even realize that they actually have the power to change the focus of their mind, and turn the page. Gaining the understanding and realization that we have the ability to change the focus of our minds is a very powerful tool for altering our mindsets.

Let's go over some examples of this, to create a better understanding. When my father, Guy, passed away, I felt an incredible sense of loss, sadness, and pain. This is where my mind went when I first heard the news. It was very negative, and it weighed heavily on my soul...until I decided to turn my focus to a different page. I began looking at how I was so blessed to have had this man in my life, and even more so as a loving father. Focusing on all of the amazing experiences we shared, the fun times, and reading all these wonderful pages in my mind, I became full of gratitude and love. Ultimately, I was joyfully smiling while there were still tears of sorrow in my eyes.

Another example of the page master mindset at work would be during a severe car crash where we were able to walk away and we weren't badly injured. Say we were in a car together driving to work one morning when we got into a serious accident where the car was totaled, our day would be severely inconvenienced, and we would be late for work. We could focus negatively on the fact that the car was destroyed and our day's schedule was all thrown off, or we could turn the page. By turning the page, we would be able to have our minds think more positively about the events like how lucky we were to be alive, and how we would live another day to see our loved ones once again.

The more we all exercise our minds, and control our page master mindsets, the easier it becomes to actually accomplish this. Don't think that just because you understand this technique, there will never be any times when bad thoughts or pages come up during life. This is just a tool to help so that when those difficult times do come, we have enough awareness to be a page master. Turn the page in your mind, and focus on other positive thoughts. This is part of having self-awareness, using *The Asset Mindset*, and being a positive influence on your own mind. Your focus definitely matters. We need to focus positively on our situations and life goals if we want them to change.

It is time to start discussing the difficulties with making changes: the steps, techniques, and where to get started. Depending on where we are with our mindsets or personal development, we may be able to answer these questions a little faster or slower. Some topics or challenges will take more or less time and energy. First off, how do we know what we need to change in our lives? Then the next step becomes, how do we initiate the change we want? Lastly, how do we stay focused, and make it happen?

Getting started can be the most frustrating step, at times. There is no momentum built up yet, and there is the issue of what direction to move in. What do you want to do during and with your life? This is a question which is all too often answered with, "I don't know" or "I want to be rich." Both of these answers are completely inadequate. We cannot be an asset to ourselves if we don't know who or what we want to become. If you already know this, then great! You are well on your way! For those of us who don't know, we need to spend some time looking inside ourselves and our thoughts. In this step, we will definitely need to spend some alone time with ourselves. We may need to journal, go for a walk, meditate, or spend some time in nature. Get away from things that distract you and sincerely spend some time, one-on-one, with your thoughts. Think of who you want to become. Where would you like to see yourself in a year, five years, ten years, or farther on down the road? We need to define ourselves and our goals. This will help us come up with a plan, and having a plan will greatly improve our chances of attaining our goals. If your goals aren't a little scary to you, then they aren't big enough. Make sure to dream big when it comes to your goals. Do not be vague, and really define your plan. As the author and life mentor Chris Hogan loves to say all the time, "Dream in HD." In other words, envision your future dreams in high definition. The better and more detailed the plan, the higher our odds are of reaching those goals.

Once we have an idea where we would like to see ourselves, then we can start backwards planning. What is backwards planning? Well, this concept of planning is when we start our plan from our end goals, and then begin from that point backwards in time, planning the steps to get there. Backwards planning is a great strategy for people who have a difficult time knowing where to start. This type of planning process is constantly used in the military, and is extremely effective. If we wanted to be on a target at 0400 (4:00 am), we would start from that time, working backwards on how long it would take us to travel there, minus the time to prepare equipment to support the mission, minus time for rehearsals, minus the time to gather the supplies needed, etc. Doing this type of planning would then give us our start time to execute the plan. Knowing when to begin the plan, and being at the right place at the right time along the way to achieve the desired end state, are crucial factors in ensuring that a mission is successful. Figure out your dreams and aspirations, set a goal, and start your planning.

One useful technique to start backwards planning would be to write out a list of all the assets we will need, and the steps we will need to take in order to reach our goal. Remember to think broadly about the assets needed. They could be resources such as people, supplies, money, education, or tools. Once we have compiled our list, we will need to estimate the time each step will take. Now that we have the steps listed with times, we will need to sequence them in reverse order to create a timeline for the goal. If any of the steps are rather large tasks on our way to reaching our goals, we should break them down into their own plan to get the task accomplished. The more we can break things down and get more detailed, the easier the plan will be to follow and achieve.

Next, is to commit to this plan by putting it out there and writing it down. It can be written out on a white board with dry erase markers, written down on a calendar, or entered into a computer or phone. Do whatever works best for you. Personally, dry erase boards have been a favorite of mine since being exposed to them in the military. We can't go into a team room and not find one. They are a great tool, because they can be quickly and very easily modified. Also, there is amazing satisfaction in crossing things off the list. Be sure to communicate your plan with others around you who are on your *Asset Mindset* team, so that they can give you feedback. They may have some really beneficial advice or suggestions to help you with the plan. Backwards planning will help guide your journey and build your confidence so that you will be able to obtain your goals.

Now, when working on a plan or goal, it is very important to have back up plans. There must be things in place so that when there is a change, or if an unforeseen event happens, we can continue moving forward to reach our objectives. Like Mike Tyson famously said, "Everyone has a plan until they get punched in the face!" Life will punch our plans in the face at some point. This is something most everyday people do not plan for or put any time into preparing for. Don't be an everyday person. Be exceptional, and plan for those punches. Have an exceptional mindset that will take you and your plans to the places you want to go. How do we plan for this?

We need to PACE ourselves. Not pace ourselves like taking our time, but PACE ourselves as in build a PACE plan. On an ODA, we had PACE plans for everything. A PACE plan is just a systematic way of having backups to backups. PACE stands for Primary, Alternate, Contingency, and Emergency. This can be applied to our lives in many ways, but let's build a simple example for our understanding. Say you and a friend want to get together over the weekend for dinner. You decide to make a plan with backups. So, while talking, you both agree to come up with a plan to touch base on Friday. Your PACE plan could look something like this: *Primary* means of communication will be to call each other on the cell phone. If you can't or don't have the time to make a call, then a text message will be sent as the *Alternate* means. If the cell phone was lost or stolen and you couldn't do either, the *Contingency* would be to send an email message. If that wasn't possible for whatever reason, the *Emergency* plan could be to just show up at the friend's house on Friday at 7:00 PM. This may seem like overkill, but if anything goes wrong, you will know exactly what to do next because there is already a plan in place.

Backup plans are very important when working towards an important objective. We may feel overwhelmed with the whole PACE plan idea, but if and when things go wrong, we will be glad we had a backup. At the very minimum, we should at least have the Primary and Alternate parts of PACE for any major planning that we do. For example, if your goal is to go to school to obtain a special degree, you probably don't want to just apply to only one school. They may not accept you, or who knows, maybe there could be a natural disaster of some sort where the school was flooded and it was permanently closed. The point being, if we already have well established backup plans when we start, it won't really affect us or slow us down very much when things go sideways. Always have some level of a PACE plan for your goals and objectives.

Having a plan is wonderful. But having a plan without motivation or real effort will get you nowhere. The plan is our vehicle, and our motivation along with our effort is the fuel that powers the plan. The more motivation and effort we put in, the faster the plan goes. Reach deep down inside yourself, put in sincere effort, and find your motivation. When things don't go as planned, it can be difficult to stay motivated. It may even make us think that it is impossible to reach our goals, or make us feel like quitting. We cannot give in to this negativity, however, or all will be lost. Keep working your plan at all costs. If you do this, you will never have any regrets, and you will most likely be very impressed with the end results you obtain.

Time to share a story about motivation. There is a true warrior and a dear friend that I have been blessed to call my brother, who we will call "Dirty." While out on a mission in Afghanistan, I was getting to know and assess a new guy who had been attached to our team. We all do this type of assessment when we are conducting operations downrange, so we have a clue to who we are working with. This man was an Airforce Combat Controller who would communicate with aircraft overhead during operations. We will call him "Mr. Airman." While getting to know each other, he mentioned a place where he had served before. Little did he know, I had someone very close to me who served at the same place during the same time. Inquiring if he knew my Green Beret brother, Dirty, he began to share a firsthand story of Dirty which did not surprise me at all. Still, the story he shared left me completely inspired and in awe because after I asked Mr. Airman if he knew Dirty, the first words out of his mouth were, "He is a F--- ing warrior!"

He then proceeded to share his eyewitness account of watching Dirty in combat, and it went like this. They were in a very bad place, and in the middle of a TIC (Troops in Contact). Dirty was manning the turret of their gun truck while Mr. Airman was in the back of the same truck, actively radioing for air support. Mr. Airman was looking up at Dirty operating the weapon system in the turret when Dirty suddenly took a round to the face! The round entered by the corner of his mouth and exited his neck by his jawbone. Then the bullet reentered his shoulder, finally exiting again from the back of Dirty's shoulder. Let's just say, this is an example of things not going as planned. Dirty could have very easily given up and lost all of his motivation after being shot in the face. He could have panicked, or fallen into the poor me victim mentality.

That's not how the story goes, though, and that is also why it is being used as an example of real motivation and effort when sticking to a plan. Ultimately, Dirty's plan was to man his weapon system and protect his brothers, no matter what the cost. Mr. Airman explained that after Dirty was shot, he immediately reached down into his individual First Aid kit, grabbed a field dressing for his wounds, opened it up, and pinned it between his bleeding neck and bloody shoulder. All this while getting back on his weapon system in the turret and returning fire. Mr. Airman said it was only a matter of seconds before Dirty was right back in the fight, manning the gun in the turret, protecting himself and his fellow soldiers: truly an amazing feat, demonstrating a true warrior's heart. Dirty made it back home to his loved ones because of his motivation and effort. He is currently retired from the military enjoying family life thanks to taking ownership of his life situations, staying motivated, and having a strong personal *Asset Mindset* .

Me with Mr. Airman after a mission.

When you are executing one of your plans and things don't go your way, don't make excuses for yourself or give up on yourself. Stay motivated, put in every ounce of effort you have, and get back to your mission or plan. If Dirty can get shot in the face and keep pushing forward with his plan, then you can push through whatever it is in your way. The key here is, you must get back to your plan. It may be a little rougher than you expected, but remember to always have your PACE plans ready to fall back on. Use *The Asset Mindset* to stay motivated and put forth your sincere effort, so that you will be able to accomplish amazing feats.

Fear is something we all will face in one way or another when it comes to executing our plan to make our dreams a reality. We need to confront fear, but at times we also need to let it go and accept that it is part of the human experience. Sharing another much less dramatic real-life story about dealing with fear while pursuing a goal, we go back to becoming an Airborne soldier. This one was personal, and it was a lesson on acceptance and trust. Now, jumping from a perfectly good airplane was something at this point in time I had never done before. Therefore, it was extremely important for me to take the Airborne training seriously. There was extreme focus during all stages of the training, and my mindset was that I was going to make sure to always do things correctly. I chose to believe that the fear of jumping from a plane would be overcome by the training, so I decided to face the fear head on.

Before doing actual live jumps from a plane during the last week of airborne school, called "Jump Week," there is a "Tower Week." Tower Week is full of rehearsals in which soldiers practice leaping from towers. During Tower Week, we hook up and jump from the towers as commanded by good old Sergeant Airborne. Well, Sergeant Airborne has lots of soldiers to get through his towers, so the pace is pretty fast. The pace is akin to trying to hurry up and get the groceries into the house as fast as you can while it is raining. While approaching the tower door, we are supposed to hook up our two risers onto our harness before exiting the 30 ft. tower. Not being very experienced, I only had one riser hooked up by the time I reached the tower door. I told Sergeant Airborne I only had one riser hooked up, and was not ready to go yet. Let's just say, that was not going to fly with him. The Black Hat looked me in the eye while I tried to get my other riser hooked up and said, "Ah, you should be fine." He proceeded to push me right out the tower door without being properly attached with both of my risers to my harness! Being perfectly honest, fear was definitely a factor in that moment. Weighing over 230 pounds, and not being a small man, the panic was the single riser holding me was going to fail! I felt like my heart missed a beat when I was launched off of the jump tower. The thinking was, since things were not hooked up correctly prior to being shoved off and out of a 30 ft. tower door, there was going to be a loud snap from the one lonely riser supporting all my weight. The snap would be followed by a loud painful thump with me smacking into the hard ground below. I had no choice but to let the fear go, and accept what was going to happen.

Thankfully, this did not happen, and the one riser connected to the harness was strong enough to get me to the ground in one piece. After landing safely, it was then time to get back in line to go up the tower and do it all over again. While climbing to the top, my adrenaline was still pumping. There was no way both risers wouldn't be hooked up before I jumped from the tower this time. Arriving at the top again, Sergeant Airborne was smiling when he saw me coming. He paused briefly from his hasty pace of getting soldiers out the tower door, and asked, "How was your last jump?"

"Not very good. There was only one riser hooked up to my harness, and I could have been seriously injured," I responded.

He replied, "Soldier, I knew you would be fine. One riser is more than enough to hold you. Have trust in the equipment, and now you know one riser is adequately strong enough to support you. You will always feel comfortable when you have two."

There was a method to Sergeant Airborne's madness, which was not initially understood. Things weren't perceived for what they really were. While I had initially just thought that he was a jerk, the experience turned into a lesson on dealing with stress, trust, accepting the situation I was in, and of course, dealing with fear and letting it go. There will always be times in life when unexpected things happen, and we will not be in control. *Do not* let fear take over. Accept the situation you are in and ride it out. When I exited out of the tower door with only one riser hooked up, I let my mind get too focused on fear, when in actuality, everything was going to be fine. Just because we think something bad is going to happen does not mean it will. The situation most likely will not be as bad as we think, and there will be lessons we can learn from the experience; unless, of course, the experience kills us, and at that point who cares. We won't have to worry anymore. Now, that is some serious letting go, and a little Special Forces humor for you.

While we are still on the topic of how things aren't always as they seem, and the ways that our perceptions can deceive us, here's an experience I will share from later in my military career. When deployed to Afghanistan, my ODA was out on a night patrol, and it was pitch dark out with no moon. The sky looked as if it was sparkling with glitter rather than stars due to our night vision optics. Our night vision didn't have perfect depth perception or clarity, but boy did the stars always look spectacular. We had been out for days, and the call was made to rest overnight, or "RON" in our current location. This wasn't really resting overnight, because it was already well past 2 am. As usual, I was in the turret pulling security again. This is something that every Special Operator takes very seriously, because the lives of your teammates are in your hands. I was scanning the surrounding area constantly looking for any threats or movement.

After a few minutes, my eyes barely catch something off in the distance and briefly move over by a large rock formation on the side of the mountain close to us. At that moment, my adrenaline and senses started going crazy, and I became completely focused on that area. I could feel every heartbeat pumping through my body, and the hair on my neck standing up.

Let me take a moment to explain what soldiers or fighters will do when it comes to making movements for conducting an attack. While trying to sneak up on a target, they will try to bound, or move from one covered and concealed position to the next, without being spotted. This is the type of movement I'm laser focused on watching for when pulling security. While scanning to observe any additional movement, sure enough there was movement bounding from that rock formation to a bush a little closer to our position. Instead of panicking and just slinging bullets in that direction, the team is immediately notified over our personal radios with, "I have movement." I give them distance and direction information while still observing the area.

The team starts preparing for contact with the enemy, and I see some more movement bounding closer to another covered position. This time it was a little odd. Another radio call goes out, "Standby, there is more movement." The next time observing the movement, there is the obvious determination that it was a large rabbit! Yes, this rabbit was doing what rabbits do. It would hop from one spot to another, then pause for a bit before hopping to the next spot to avoid predators. Of course, the next call out over the radio was not my proudest moment. After telling the team to "Stand down, it's just a rabbit," there were a few smartass comments about me being scared of a rabbit etc. "Watch out for Peter Cottontail!" This was completely appropriate for the situation, and I would have done the same thing if on the other side of the radio. Once again, we were using humor to get through a stressful time. After a few of these remarks, I quickly came back over the radio, "Hey, if a rabbit can't sneak up on our RON site, then you all know the bad guys won't be able to!" The radio response was, "Very true." Also, to be honest, the term "bad guys" wasn't used, but you get the point.

A quick picture while pulling Security

This is the type of detail and awareness we need to apply in our lives. Keep a watchful eye out for everything that's going on around you. Yes, we may get spun up a little at times, and think we are in a certain situation when we are actually not. There is an advantage to this, though; by being so focused and aware of what's going on, we won't miss out on an opportunity if it rears its head. People may make some wise comments to us, but they will respect our efforts, plans, and the focus we have on our goals. Again, things may not be what you thought they were, but it is better to be prepared with some sort of plan than just lay back and letting life happen around you. Ignorance may be bliss as some say, but ignorance does not create success or opportunity. If we want success, we must stay alert and remain extremely focused on our life plans, while at the same time being ready to make changes when appropriate. This is *The Asset Mindset* philosophy: you need to put in action to create the life you desire.

Chapter 10

Opportunity and Creating Success

Flames were flying up in the air, and I could feel the heat blasting across my entire body. Loud explosions were going off and ringing in my ears. People were screaming wildly right in front of me, and it was hard to see with all the flashing lights. The smell of all the smoke was so strong I could taste it in the back of my throat.

This was not a scene from my combat experience, but the view from on stage looking out across thousands of screaming concert goers. When the encore from the concert ended, it would soon be time to get ready to move to the limousine and off to the airport to leave in a private jet. I wondered, how in the world did I get here, and get to experience such amazing things?

It was all because of my greatest asset: me. Don't get me wrong; I didn't do it alone, and this definitely wasn't my concert. Still, it was through my own actions and choices that I found myself with opportunity, and in that place in time. I created doors, and then I walked through those open doors of opportunity. I said "Yes" to make them happen.

The lesson? Be your own greatest asset. Seek out doors of opportunity in your life, whether you have to make them or find them. When you do this, you too will experience amazing things which will have you, too, asking yourself, "How did I get here?"

This chapter of life all started on a beautiful white sandy beach, right after I had gotten off of active duty from the military. While walking on this tropical Bahamas beach, I heard music playing off in the distance. Being curious, and looking for a fun place to hang out, the decision was made to go check it out. I found that it was coming from a famous rock star's private cabana, a guy who is an American Badass, a patriot, and who strongly supports the troops. The one and only Kid Rock from Detroit, Michigan! Having served in the military, and knowing about his past USO tours supporting the troops, I decided to go up and say something.

"Excuse me, Kid Rock. I want to thank you for all you do going overseas and showing support for the troops. We really appreciate it, and it means more than you will ever know!" I said.

"You're welcome, and are you in the military now?" Kid Rock responded.

"Actually, I just got off active duty two weeks ago," I said.

"What brings you down to the Bahamas?" he asked.

"I came here to celebrate my birthday because last year I spent my birthday doing missions in Afghanistan."

"Well, have a seat and let me buy you a birthday drink then to celebrate!" he said.

Little did I know how that decision to go up to Kid Rock and say thank you would drastically change the next two years of my life, and continue to impact my life even to the present day.

You see, I was full of gratitude, giving thanks to him for all his military support. At the same time, he was full of gratitude for my service. At first, he didn't even know what I did while serving in the military. It wasn't until later that night, and after some festivities, that he was able to get me to spill the beans that I was a Special Forces Green Beret when I served in the Army. In the beginning, there was just genuine gratitude for my military service to our country. Next thing you know, we were hanging out having some drinks, and then some food, and then one thing led to another, and another. We ended up having dinner together and going to a casino, sharing stories, and having a blast! It made for a truly amazing day, and birthday experience that only came to an end when the sun started coming up the next morning. Just as I was leaving Kid Rock's hotel suite, who will be referred to as "Rock" from now on, he said, "Do it again tomorrow?"

At that moment, I was stunned. I of course responded, "You bet!" In true rock star fashion, the festivities went on to last for three consecutive days, and after really getting to know each other, there was lots of mutual respect. A genuine friendship had developed between us. Rock asked if I had a job lined up after getting out of the military, and my response was, "No, not yet."

"Well, I may have something for you," he replied. Long story short, the next two years were spent working with Rock. We have been across the world together, and I have been so blessed to experience things most people would think only happen in the movies. Heck, he even stood up as one of my groomsmen at my wedding.

This story wasn't shared to boast about myself, and how cool I am because of who I know. Being a Green Beret, I already know I'm cool. This is an inside joke among us Green Berets, by the way. We like to say that our number one rule is to always be and look cool. It's an inside joke in our community, because we frequently get into really crazy, bad, or awkward situations where we just need to try our best to look cool, like we have everything together. No matter what, though, you should never think you're too cool to laugh at yourself.

The Kid Rock story was mentioned to demonstrate how putting yourself out there, having gratitude, and taking initiative can change the course of our lives and create incredible experiences. In my case, these attributes all created a unique opportunity, and both Rock and I took notice. He didn't have to hire me at all, and I didn't have to work for him. However, we connected because something else was there. What we shared was a similar mindset, and it was *The Asset Mindset*. Obviously, Rock wasn't a Special Forces Green Beret, and by no means am I a rock star musician. Yet, we could relate on so many levels. Rock's work ethic, motivation, and discipline had brought him to an elite level of musical success most people can't even imagine obtaining. This is very similar in so many ways to achieving the elite level of being a Special Forces Operator. It is *The Asset Mindset,* where we are going to do whatever it takes to succeed and get to where we want to be in life. Rock most definitely has it, as well.

This also reflects another major point in this book, which is: you DO NOT need to be a member of Special Forces to have *The Asset Mindset*. You too can have it, create it, and apply it in your life. Rock was his own greatest asset to achieving his success, constantly working and pushing himself to be better. I was amazed by the amount of effort and time he put into all his music and shows. Good enough was never good enough. You, too, need to be your own greatest asset, and do these exact same things in order to obtain *The Asset Mindset,* so that you can have success and achieve your dreams.

Rock also does something that is essential to *The Asset Mindset*: he surrounds himself with positive people. Everyone in his Twisted Brown Trucker Band, also known as "TBT", are all positive assets, or else they wouldn't be there. Just like on an ODA, your teammates become your extended family. The same goes for Kid Rock and the Twisted Brown Trucker Band. They are all part of the Kid Rock family, which I was blessed to become a part of. It also made my transition from being active duty on an ODA back to civilian life much smoother than anticipated. It's important to note, Rock will not tolerate subpar standards, and this resonates with what we discussed earlier, about building your positive team of asset mindset peers. A favorite quote which was used countless times, and still is used by Rock, goes, "When you find good people, you keep them close!" This mirrors exactly one of the key characteristics of having *The Asset Mindset* .

Hanging in a limo with Mr. Kid Rock.

Another factor involved with opportunity and creating success is being able to seize the opportunities that are put in front of us. If we never say "Yes" to an offer, or apply for that dream job, we will definitely miss out. Do nothing, and we will get nothing in return. We must put ourselves out there into the world to create opportunities. If I didn't say yes to the Army, or yes to Rock, then so many incredible life-changing experiences would have been missed. Take chances to go after success and your dreams, just like this saying suggests, "No risk, no reward!" We have to take risks when opportunities arise, because we can't always go back to try and seize the same opportunity all over again. That moment in time has passed. Don't be afraid to say "Yes" and seize those special moments in life that come along. Stay aware and alert for opportunities which come along in your life, so you can seize them. We need to pay attention, and put ourselves out there. Put yourself in positive environments that create opportunities for you. Spend time in these environments, and get to know people in them. In a sense, you need to go where the action is! Go to where your dreams can come true.

The author Ken Colman has a book specifically on this topic, called, "The Proximity Principle." This book goes into great detail about putting ourselves in the right place to create opportunities for our dreams to come true. Set yourself up to create and seize the moments of opportunity that come before you, and you can achieve success like never before. Yes, we are powerful with an *Asset Mindset*, but we must be humble. A smart person knows they do not know everything. As always, be careful of the "Know-it-all" types out there, because they obviously aren't truly intelligent. Like Dad always said, "A little bit of knowledge can be a dangerous thing." We have all been there at some point during our life where we thought we knew something, and it turned out to be otherwise. Stay humble, and listen to people with experience who have walked the path before you. They can tell us about obstacles to avoid, or better yet, maybe some shortcuts. This was another nugget gifted to me by my father. It has paid huge dividends in life, from times in school, to times in my military career. I owe much of my success while being a Special Forces Operator to this advice given to me at a young age. Being humble, and wise with *The Asset Mindset*, will set you up for success.

While going through the training pipeline to get qualified as a Green Beret, I searched out mentors and Cadre who had been there, and done it. I picked their brains, and asked them to share as many tips and tricks as possible to be a successful team member. Over ninety nine percent of the time, they were more than eager to share. Most people who are successful in their career or life are very happy to help. It gives them joy so don't be afraid to talk to them and get advice. We should always continue to learn throughout our lives, stay humble, and seek out successful people we want to learn from. When you find these successful people, start picking their brains, and show them lots of gratitude. They will be an incredible asset for your future success.

Meeting successful and positive people from all walks of life allows us to gather nuggets of knowledge. Lots of people refer to these pieces of knowledge as nuggets, because they are as valuable as nuggets of gold. These nuggets of knowledge can be amazingly helpful in our life journeys. They can be shortcuts or techniques allowing us to reach our goals faster.

They can be words of wisdom which can help us deal with obstacles in life. We have covered a few nuggets already, such as, "People may victimize us in life, but they can't keep us in a victim mentality," and having a "How do I?" mentality. Think back through this book, and reflect on the nuggets you've found which resonate with you. Different nuggets touch different people in different ways. Then think back to the nuggets you have received previously in your life from loved ones and mentors.

Life is full of these nuggets of knowledge. We just need to keep our eyes and ears open for them. Write them down, take notes, and start collecting new ones to help with your motivation and focus. Nuggets can also be advice on what to do, or where to go to accomplish a goal; for example, if you need to attend a certain school, or acquire a certain skill. Understanding these nuggets can also help us create a mindset leading us to take action towards making our dreams come true. Continue to build *The Asset Mindset* within yourself with these golden nuggets of knowledge to create the life you want to live.

The next move is to realize that everyone's path is different, and everyone has problems to deal with along their life journey. It is how we deal with the crap we encounter along the way in life that determines whether we prosper or not! When dealing with life's problems, which everyone encounters at some point, it's very important to take ownership of our life's situations. Most of the time, when we are dealing with our life problems, no one is going to magically come along and rescue us from them. It will most likely require our own motivation, focus, and determination to get ourselves out of the problems, and get cleaned up. I understand it is difficult at times, and sometimes while stuck knee deep in the crap, we have to walk up to our waists in it to get out of it. This really sucks as a metaphor, but in Special Forces this is a reality we face sometimes.

My Green Beret brother Ryan had this become his reality as he was stuck in a ditch full of human feces during a combat deployment fighting for his life. He can literally talk about being in the *shit* when he shares a war story! Remember this the next time you think your life situation stinks. You can learn more about this event in his book, *Tip of The Spear.* Being stuck in a crappy situation wasn't just a metaphor for him, and he had to fight his way out. But nevertheless, when we are in an extremely poor situation we need to get out. Make it happen and find your way out, even if you have to wade through neck-deep crap to get it done. The main focus is for us to get ourselves out. Otherwise, we may be waiting for a very long time to get help, or even worse, spending the rest of our lives in a pile of crap! You are, once again, your own best asset for resolving these problems. Understand that you are on your own life path. You *will* get dirty, as everyone does, but having the proper mindset will be a huge advantage for overcoming problems and cleaning up your life.

If we want to create success, we must be willing to make a change. Change will never happen if you don't *make changes!* If we keep going to the same job we hate, and do not pursue a new one, then whose fault is it that we are stuck? If we want to be healthy, then we need to make changes for a healthy lifestyle. Nobody can do exercises for us, or eat properly for us. You are your own greatest asset! Remember this: you control and contribute to your situation in life more than anyone or anything else does. You need to make changes in your life to improve it.

At this very moment, if you stop and think for a second, you know deep down inside of some changes you could make to start improving your life immediately. Focus on these changes, prioritize them, write them down, and act in a manner to facilitate these changes you want. The good news is, you are actively seeking change right now by reading this book and working towards personal growth. Keep the positive momentum going, and capitalize on everything you can. Otherwise, the changes you really want in life won't happen, because the changes you truly want are up to you to create.

As discussed earlier, a huge part of making changes is being aware of opportunities and taking advantage of them. These opportunities can be referred to as doors of opportunity that may open up for us. These doors can be open, closed, or even cracked open just a little bit when we encounter them. Do not just walk by the doors without at least checking them out. You owe it to yourself to at least explore them by peeking your head in a little to see what's on the other side. Many people have opportunities which show up in their life, but they never take the time to check the door to see what may be on the other side. Do not do this, because it could turn out to be a missed opportunity. The one sticking point about time is that we can never go backwards in it. We can try to go back to an opportunity, but the timing will never be the same. Thus, it will never be the exact same opportunity. The initial opportunity will be forever lost. Opportunities must be taken advantage of when they present themselves if we want to create change and maximize our prospects.

Imagine you are in the river of life and you are about to be swept over the edge of a massive waterfall where certain death will result! Suddenly, someone miraculously tosses you a rope to grab on to. Do you grab that rope, or just think about it? Of course, you grasp that lifeline and hold on with all you've got! You should do the same thing when golden opportunities present themselves. Grab them and don't let go! Doing this could save your dreams, or even better, make them come true.

When an opportunity is placed in front of us in life, we need to explore it right away before the time window is closed, and the opportunity is locked shut forever. To quote the heavyweight boxer Ed Latimore, "Wait too long and life will pass you by. Don't make the mistake of thinking everything will give you a second chance." If we want to play a professional sport, we really need to start that journey before we are 40 or 50 years old, right? Also, opportunity does not always come easily. If the door is just cracked open, we may need to make the effort to force it open the rest of the way. Every opportunity still requires work, effort, and motivation to make the most of it. Be willing to do these things, and you will reap the benefits. Some people in our lives may be assets who show us the door, or even open it for us, but we still need to act and walk ourselves through it. Opportunities always do, and will definitely continue to cross your path during your life's journey. Keep an eye out for them, hunt them down, and be willing to pursue them relentlessly if you want to create a successful positive change.

Chapter 11

Key Characteristics of *The Asset Mindset* Philosophy

No one influences your life more than you do, positively or negatively. You are your own greatest asset! Having a powerful mindset and understanding this philosophy allows us to be the greatest asset to ourselves. That is why I titled this book, *The Asset Mindset*. Once you realize that you are your own greatest asset in your life, and you put the philosophy into action, it is only then that you will have *The Asset Mindset*. This philosophy creates an extremely powerful mindset. You are taking ownership of your life, and giving yourself the power of creation to build your life and dreams the way you desire. Don't get me wrong; there are most definitely external factors which come into play in life such as luck, both good and bad. Nevertheless, it is completely possible to overcome bad luck or unforeseen circumstances with *The Asset Mindset*.

Recall Romy and what he has accomplished after the bad luck he had getting shot in the neck becoming paralyzed. Dreams and achievements do not come true on their own. We need to *act* to make them happen. Even getting rich the quick and lazy way by winning the lottery still requires us to act and buy the ticket. This technique is not recommended, of course, as the odds are completely stacked against us. Remember, we want to have more control and ownership of our success. We need to show up! Your actions will always influence and create your destiny more than anything else does. So take control of this powerful tool, and live with *The Asset Mindset* philosophy.

Positive behavior is a key characteristic of *The Asset Mindset,* which can be observed in anyone who achieves success in life after adopting this philosophical mindset. They will have productive habits, and behave in such a way that they can't help but foster positivity. These successful Asset Mindset people are leaders and role models to others. Their behaviors inspire others, and demonstrate to others that they can create success in their own lives as well. Think of anyone who is successful, and you will find positive behavior and *The Asset Mindset* philosophy. These are interconnected in such a way that you can't really have one without the other. If you apply *The Asset Mindset* philosophy in your life, creating positive behaviors and habits, then you can become incredibly successful in your life, too.

A key characteristic we must have if we are going to obtain *The Asset Mindset* is self-awareness. We need to be aware of the goals, desires, and dreams of success that we want to create. We must have the self-awareness to know our own strengths and weaknesses. If we do not have this self-awareness, then how are we supposed to get anywhere? It would be similar to floating aimlessly through life, like a ship drifting out at sea without a rudder. We need to take the helm, and steer the ship; otherwise, we are at the mercy of the forces around us.

Do not let your life be at the mercy of the forces around you. Have the self-awareness to steer your life towards your dreams and goals. Your life is your ship, *The Asset Mindset* you are developing is the rudder for your ship of life, and you are the Captain! Don't worry if you have veered off course a little, or even been going in the wrong direction. Being the Captain gives you the ability to right the ship and turn it around at any point in your life. Self-awareness is a must when employing *The Asset Mindset* philosophy in your life.

Managing self-awareness is crucial to effectively creating it. Spend time looking at where you are and the situations around you. Spend time with yourself, focusing on your goals and how to get there. You need to constantly monitor your self-awareness and adjust accordingly. Find your weaknesses and learn how to manage them or, better yet, eliminate them. Realize your strengths, and leverage them in such a way that they are most effective for maximizing your results. Give yourself alone time, write things down, pray on it, meditate, keep a journal; do whatever it takes to manage and maintain your self-awareness. We should all do this daily to avoid accidentally drifting aimlessly in life. Own who you are and who you want to be. The management practice of your self-awareness is a must to achieve the success you desire.

Moving beyond self-awareness comes relationship awareness. Having relationship awareness is another characteristic of *The Asset Mindset* philosophy. Be aware of your relationships with others. How do these relationships affect your life? Remember, we want to build a strong and positive *Asset Mindset* team around us. These relationships will take time and effort, but they will be very rewarding and can help us in unimaginable ways. While working on our relationship awareness, we need to be cognizant of any negative relationships we may have. Negative relationships can be extremely detrimental to our dreams and our successes. These negative relationships need to be turned into positive ones, or we will need to cut away completely. Letting go of the relationship may be necessary. To borrow another lesson from my time as an Airborne soldier, when we are jumping out of a plane and the main parachute is messed up or malfunctions, we don't waste time on it. We move on. We cut away, and pull the reserve parachute, because we know we don't have time to waste in the air trying to fix something that is already broken. If we spent time trying to fix the problem, we would end up crashing and burning into the ground, because there is only so much time available to get things right.

This goes the same for our relationships and life, because we only have so much time to get things right. It may be painful and it may be scary, but cutting away bad relationships is a must in order to achieve our highest potential. Otherwise, these negative relationships will be like extra anchors thrown overboard, dragging on our ship. Meanwhile, we will be at the helm desperately trying to steer our lives in the direction we want to go without getting the results we desire. When establishing your own Asset Mindset philosophy, you must continually have awareness of the relationships around you.

Proper management needs to be applied to our relationship awareness, just as in our self-awareness. There must be time and effort put into these relationships. Existing relationships must be maintained, and new ones should be established that support our abilities to create success and attain our goals. Don't be afraid to reach out and rekindle old positive relationships as well. We should be constantly seeking out new positive asset relationships, while trying to improve and honor the current positive asset relationships we already have. Managing these relationships properly will create opportunities, and further enhance our ability to make positive things happen in our lives. It is much easier to sail a ship with a crew than to do it all alone. Just make sure you have a good solid crew, not a bunch of drunken seasick sailors around you. Properly applying management skills to your relationship awareness and self-awareness is a characteristic of using *The Asset Mindset* philosophy.

Having the ability to make good choices is another key characteristic of having *The Asset Mindset*. Everyone needs to make choices in life to create the success they desire, and the more we have *The Asset Mindset* philosophy the easier it becomes to make these correct choices. While observing situations in life with the perspective of *The Asset Mindset* these situational choices will become easier to see as either a positive or negative asset for you. This clearer vision occurs through your mental focus and the self-awareness characteristics built through having a positive mindset. Everybody has to make choices; even doing nothing at all is still a choice. The stronger we build *The Asset Mindset* philosophy within us, the better the choices we will make.

When we have a vision of success, we have direction; when we have both of these things in place, then we have answers. Attaining the right answers for your life direction only makes your choices easier and more productive. For example, if you want to be a Green Beret, then the choice to join the Army and go to Special Forces Assessment and Selection is a no-brainer. It's similar to setting directions for a destination with the GPS in your phone or car. Once you set the destination, you will have a clear path to follow. Your route options and turns to take automatically get narrowed down. Some choices are obvious, and other ones you may weigh. This road is shorter, but it gets backed up at certain times of day, and so forth; these are all considerations that you will make as you navigate your path. Answers will come to you once you have narrowed down the problem set.

Having the vision and goal of where you want to be will make the choices for getting there much simpler. Of course, this doesn't mean we will never have any tough choices to make in life. *The Asset Mindset* does not magically make everything easy, but it sure will help with making the correct choices for our successes easier. It will increase the odds of making the best possible choice for you, along with being able to live with the consequences of your choices. Developing the ability to make better choices in your life is definitely a characteristic of *The Asset Mindset.*

The beliefs or belief system of someone who has *The Asset Mindset* philosophy is something that is shared by many successful people from all walks of life, all around the world. One of the main foundational beliefs we will find within these successful people is the belief that they control their own destiny. They know that no one else contributes more to their success than they do, both positively or negatively. We must build, and always maintain, these same beliefs inside ourselves if we are to have *The Asset Mindset.* Another important belief for us to always have is that we need to work hard for what we want. If you really want to achieve something, you will find a way--and if you do not, you will find yourself some sort of excuse. Recall that we avoid making excuses when we have *The Asset Mindset.* Successful people understand this concept, and they are willing to work hard putting in the time and effort to create their future success.

Successful people have *The Asset Mindset* philosophy and share similar beliefs, which in turn allows them to achieve their goals. They tend to have a greater belief in gratitude, being grateful for where they are in life's journey. This gratitude tends to lead to more happiness and fulfillment in life. People with *The Asset Mindset* also believe that it is important to surround themselves with the right people for supporting their dreams. As Kid Rock has repeatedly told me, "When you find good people, you keep them close." Going through life with a mindset full of gratitude will make you happier and facilitate stronger relationships with others. Gratitude also aids in the development of positive opportunities for your dreams to come true.

Additionally, there is the belief within successful people that they need to constantly learn and grow as they journey through life. This is something that we must do as well if we are to progress to success. There are many different ways to be successful in this world, and many accomplished people share similar beliefs to obtain success. These similar beliefs are absolutely common among countless prosperous people all around the world. Those people all have and use *The Asset Mindset* in their lives to focus on positive progress, personal growth, finding joy in life, and creating success. These beliefs are some of the key characteristics of having *The Asset Mindset* philosophy. We can practice these same beliefs, apply them to create our own successes, and in turn, create more happiness in our lives. Nothing and no one can stop you from building these exact same beliefs and applying them to your life goals.

Another key characteristic of *The Asset Mindset* is that there is focus on the future. This future focus is essential to achieving success. We need to know where we want to take our lives, and where we want to be. If we are constantly reliving the past, and always talking about times gone by, then we are not being productive. We must leave the past behind us no matter what it is, and focus our minds towards our future. This doesn't mean that you need to forget the past completely, because we all learn from our past experiences. It just means that the past should not be your main focus. A great analogy to make sense of this concept is something that I once heard from Mr. Dave Ramsey of Ramsey Solutions in the Nashville, Tennessee area: there is a reason the rearview mirror in your car is so small compared to the windshield. In other words, we need to be looking forward and paying more attention to what is in front of us, so we can get where we want to go. If we spend too much time looking in the rearview mirror, we will go off the road. It is the same way in life. If we spend too much time focused on our past, we will go off track, distracted from accomplishing our future dreams and goals. Staying attentively focused on your future is the only way to create the future you want.

Keeping focused on our future goals may seem overwhelming at times, or it may appear to be a very long road. Do not let this get you down. Understand that when you start living with *The Asset Mindset,* you will always be moving forward. As Chris Hogan, author of "Everyday Millionaire" likes to say, "I am Focused and not finished!" This is exactly how you will also live your life once you have completely adopted *The Asset Mindset* philosophy. Every day that we wake up, we get a chance to change, be different, and improve. Our past is our past, so let's leave it behind us where it belongs. Get on with your change and your future today. Even if you are only able to make it an inch closer to your goal on any given day, it is still closer than you were when you woke up. Focusing on the past, or doing a mile of talking, won't get us any closer to our goals compared to the inch of effort and groundwork we can make. Inches add up to feet, and feet add up quickly to getting us closer to where we want to be. Recall the discussion of using time as a proper asset and force multiplier. One inch multiplied by three-hundred-sixty-five days will bring you over thirty feet closer to your goals. Just think about it: that's with only achieving one inch of movement a day. With your focus and utilizing *The Asset Mindset* philosophy, you will most likely have lots of days which will bring you a lot closer than just one inch a day! Do not get overwhelmed by the distance you need to travel, because the more you achieve over time, the greater speed and momentum you will create towards reaching your goals.

Chapter 12

How to Bring all the Elements Together for Success

The Asset Mindset philosophy covers many thoughts, beliefs, and perspectives on life, to a level where the philosophy becomes all encompassing. There are many overlapping themes when we start putting *The Asset Mindset* all together. You will start to see this as we review the many topics we have covered, and most likely you have picked up on quite a few already. One thing is for sure: to be in Special Forces, you need to have *The Asset Mindset*. However, you don't have to be Special Forces to have *The Asset Mindset*. When you develop it and apply it, you will have the same types of success accomplishing your objectives as Green Berets and other successful people have every day, all around the world. These same thoughts, beliefs, and perspectives from *The Asset Mindset* philosophy need to be all encompassing within you, and within your life.

To begin, we need to mentally prepare and believe in ourselves. Focus on *you,* and look deep inside yourself so that you can make a choice, deciding what you want out of life. We need to get motivated and have discipline. Spend lots of time with yourself looking at your life, praying, meditating, searching inside yourself, and working to identify the "what," the "why," and the "how" necessary in order for you to become this future successful version of yourself. You and your mind are the most powerful and creative assets you have in your life. Use them wisely to prepare yourself for your future, and build *The Asset Mindset* within you.

Along life's path, we need to avoid negative environments, people, and excuses which will be detrimental to our journeys toward success. Pay close attention to your inner voice or gut feelings, because most of the time they are spot on. If you're ever confused about whether someone or something is actually a negative influence on your life, do not forget to step back. Observe the situation through a filter of love. Love is a great indicator. Are these people loving and supportive, or are they bringing you down? Is the environment positive or toxic? Is the love conditional and manipulative? If authentic love and support are not present, having viewed the situation through a perspective of love will allow you to determine the true form of your situation. When genuine love and support do not exist, you need to walk away and avoid these situations. It is your life, and you need to know what negatives to avoid so that you can follow your path to success.

Another must: avoid falling into the trap of having a victim mentality. If you currently feel this way, or if you are ever moving in this direction mentally, it is crucial that you remember the following. We often cannot control whether people or events victimize us in life. However, they CANNOT keep us in a victim mentality. Only we and our minds have the power to do that to ourselves. Be an asset to yourself, and do not allow yourself to become your own worst enemy by allowing yourself to fall into a victim's mentality!

Remember also to avoid all the talkers in life. Don't waste your time with them. Find the people who are doers and who are making great things happen in the world. Surround yourself with these positive people, emulate them, and be that type of person yourself. Be a person who walks the walk, and avoids the talker just talking. Stay away from negative environments, people, and excuses. Remember the analogy of thinking of your mind as a sponge. If your sponge was previously filled with clean water and gets dropped into a poor environment like the mud, when you pick it up, it will not be nearly as dirty. It is much harder for the impurities of the mud to penetrate into a clean saturated sponge. Thus, if your brain is already full with a positive mindset, then it is much harder for negative situations to infiltrate your mind and bring you down. If you do find yourself in a negative environment be cautious and avoid being in that dirty environment too long as the muddy water could eventually work its way in. Ideally, you really want to avoid negative influences and surroundings in your life, but we all know that is not always possible so stay positive.

When we encounter life's obstacles or deal with negative situations, the good news is that we now know how to overcome them with *The Asset Mindset*. The different life obstacles we all face come in big and small sizes, and may take a while to overcome, but we can do it. Remember, it all starts with believing in yourself, and taking ownership of the problem. By owning it, you can fix it. Show up, and be persistent when doing something to fix it. If you have fear, make sure to control your mind and focus on the positive things. Fear is an opportunity to be brave and courageous, which can lead to greatness. Again, be persistent and don't quit. Water carves through rock all by using the power of persistence. Our obstacles or problems may be as hard as a rock, but we can persist with *The Asset Mindset*. Do not let doubt step in and tell you that you can't. Have the "How do I?" attitude, and you will overcome it. These obstacles will build growth in us, and it will be painful at times. Everyone has growing pains in life, so you are not alone. Most pain is temporary, and once you overcome the obstacle the pain is gone. Putting *The Asset Mindset* philosophy into action will allow you to mentally overcome any obstacle or situation.

These different life obstacles will provide an environment for growth, and will influence our futures. The experience we gain from difficult times will teach us valuable lessons. Just as the mentors from your past and those you have yet to encounter will greatly influence your life journey, make sure to seek out new learning experiences, and seek out new lessons to learn which will also add to your personal growth. Listen for words of wisdom that can help influence your life in a positive way. Recall the Dragon Warrior Code we covered earlier for example, and how it can be so influential. There are many influential codes, creeds, prayers, and lots of other words of wisdom to live by. Find one, or many that resonate with you and try to live by them. They can be very strong influences which provide a stable foundation for your beliefs in life. These influences can be a source of great strength, giving us the ability to grow and create your own powerful *Asset Mindset*.

This education from our experiences and mentors will help us understand how to win at life. Knowing how to win is not overly complicated, but it does take motivation, dedication, and a serious work ethic. It is similar to knowing that it's easy to lose weight through diet and exercise. The challenge isn't so much in gaining the knowledge of what to do; the hard work comes with having the discipline to execute your plan. You must execute to win. Preparation and hard work are keys to winning. Remember, a battle is won, even before the battle takes place, because of those keys to winning. We need to have a serious work ethic and put in the time so that we can win in the future.

Winning later on in life starts right now with our mindset. We need to give our all to life, and never quit reaching for our goals. Again, never quit! Technically, if we never quit, we can never really lose or be defeated. When we do this, we can reach elite levels of success in our lives, just as others before us have with *The Asset Mindset*. Nobody knows how far you can take winning in your life, but wouldn't you like to find out? You are the only one who can do it, so show up and start winning with your improved mindset!

When it comes to creating transformation in our lives, there are steps and beliefs which can be extremely beneficial. To start with, we need to embrace where we are in life no matter where that may be, and own it. Then, we need to focus our hearts and minds to find the spark or calling that is deep inside of us. This will allow us to discover what it is we want to become or do. Once this step is achieved, it only becomes a matter of doing it. How to do it leads us to seek out the answers by getting educated, and learning what things must be done to make these positive changes happen. Have a positive mindset and lots of heart, just like Littleman and every other successful person who pushes through obstacles to achieve the transformational goals they desire. Be the creator of your life's success. Again, own your life, have a positive mindset, and remember your transformation only stops when you stop trying. Make sure you have thick skin, so when things get difficult you can handle the blows while continuing to push forward in the direction of your goals. Embracing *The Asset Mindset* philosophy will allow you to transform your life into the rewarding success you want it to be.

Our *Asset Mindset* teammates are the next best thing, other than our own minds, for building a successful dream life. They can guide us, help keep us on track, and teach us ways to realize our dreams faster. They will inspire us, and make us better in every way. *Asset Mindset* teammates lift us up and support us, whether they are lifelong teammates, or just temporary teammates. Build your team up as big and strong as you can, because having a positive team around you to support you will be an incredible asset for your success! Remember, true *Asset Mindset* teammates are reliable and supportive, with trust, confidence, honesty, and loyalty; they are people who will always maintain quality communications with you. If they do not meet these criteria, then they are not truly your teammates, and you do not need them around you. When you find good teammates, keep them close! You are also part of this *Asset Mindset* team, so be sure to return the favor and do all of these things for them as well. Give back to your team, and you will be amazed at the return on your investment. The number one thing you possess is your own properly trained mind, so own it and use it. Nonetheless, *The Asset Mindset* team you create will be the second-best thing you can have to create a positive and successful life for yourself.

Focusing on another major factor in your life, you must develop habits which can create success. Our behavior is key to our success. We must have positive habits to create positive results. We reap what we sow. People have known about this for thousands of years, and it is often referred to as karma. When we create positive habits, we are creating positive changes in our lives which will give us the results we desire. Positive habits feed your dreams like fertilizer feeds a plant. It makes them grow! The behaviors or habits we continuously want to practice and maintain are: use time wisely, read, learn, exercise, sleep properly, conduct our life After Action Reviews (AARs), and of course, spend time in positive environments with positive people. Stick with these categories of habits and see what works best for you. Additionally, seek out any other positive habits to aid and support you on your life journey. These positive habits are a crucial part of having and applying *The Asset Mindset* in our lives. The rewards of creating positive habits will undoubtedly make your life better and seriously increase the odds for your success.

To achieve success, we must *plan* for our successes. We have to build ourselves a road map to get where we want to go. Remember to use backwards planning to develop a solid plan which focuses on your desired outcome. Don't forget to have your Primary, Alternate, Contingency, and Emergency or "PACE" plans ready as well, for when life throws you an unforeseen event or obstacle. We definitely can count on life throwing curveballs at us randomly during our journeys. When planning, our mental focus matters, and we need to be as detailed as possible. Create lists, and make schedules and timelines to help you do whatever you need to do to get organized. Maintain and track your plan's progress. No one can plan our successes for us, so we need to make the plan for ourselves. Yes, there are people who can help you with your plan, but ultimately, it's your life and your plan. We also want to consistently try and improve our plans as we grow and learn. No one will nurture your life plan more than you. This is all part of having *The Asset Mindset* philosophy where you need to take ownership of your life plan, because you are your greatest asset.

While using *The Asset Mindset* and working our plans, opportunities will come along. We need to say "yes" when they do, so that we can seize them to pursue our dreams. Sometimes, the opportunity that presents itself can lead to a wonderful experience that we hadn't even dreamed of. An example is my two years of traveling the world working with Kid Rock as his personal security, and other mind-blowing relationships which resulted from just saying "yes" to seize a moment of opportunity. Put yourself out there in the appropriate situations and environments where your dreams can come true. Spend time in these places with the people who are there, and you may even get some new *Asset Mindset* teammates to assist you in your journey to success.

As we covered earlier, "Go to where the action is!" We need to be in an environment that is conducive for our dreams to come true. If we want to be a great boxer, we need to spend time in the boxing ring, right? Take some risks, because doing nothing is sure to result in nothing happening.

Stay alert, and keep an eye out for any opportunities which may cross your path in life. You need to go explore outside your norms, if you want results outside of the norms! Avoid the insanity trap where you are doing the exact same things day after day and expecting a better and different result. We must push ourselves to explore outside our normal comfort zones, if we want to achieve success beyond our normal results. Don't be normal, because you deserve better than normal. Decide to act when a door opens up with an opportunity for you. Sometimes, we need to push on the door to get it all the way open. But if we really want the opportunity on the other side, we must get through it one way or another. Work your plan by using *The Asset Mindset* to seize the opportunities you want in life which will bring you closer to success and your dreams.

It is time to review a list of the key elements and concepts of *The Asset Mindset,* getting down to the basic fundamentals in a "Things to do" quick and easy reference guide on the following pages. This guide is for you to copy or print out, make your own sticky notes from, or just rip it out of the book if you want. Take and use the entire list, or cut it up into the pieces that speak to you personally. Then post these key concepts in visible places to serve as a constant reminder for you to stay focused with *The Asset Mindset* philosophy!

The Asset Mindset **Things to Do :**

- Believe in yourself.
- Take ownership of your life.
- Use time wisely.
- Be and get mentally prepared.
- Be a creator.
- Find the sparks inside for your callings.
- Control your thoughts.
- Show up, be motivated, and have discipline.
- Focus on the positive.
- Remember, fear is an opportunity for bravery, courage, and greatness.
- Be focused, have heart, and never quit!
- Have a strong work ethic.
- Follow your inner guidance.
- Be a "Page Master" in difficult times.
- Be a doer, not a talker.
- Keep learning and growing.
- Find mentors in life.
- Collect nuggets of knowledge.
- Avoid negative environments, people, and excuses.
- Do not have a victim mentality.
- Be aware of the love in your life.
- Have gratitude.
- Be a giver.
- Have the "How do I?" mentality.
- Embrace the suck, and have thick skin.
- Make "To do" lists, and stay focused.
- Stay dedicated to your goals.
- Behavior matters.
- Create and maintain positive habits: Read, Exercise, Eat Healthy, etc.
- Build an Asset Mindset team of people around you.
- Make plans for your future/ Backwards planning, and PACE.
- Have awareness and conduct AARs.
- Seize and create your opportunities.
- Be your greatest asset!

The Asset Mindset is a philosophy; an understanding in which we are our own most powerful, influential, and creative asset for becoming successful in our lives. *The Asset Mindset* is a state of mind and an awareness such that we will look at ourselves and the world around us from a viewpoint where everything and everyone in our lives should be a positive asset. You need to apply this belief to your thoughts, habits, environments, and relationships with others, while at the same time focusing your energies on being a positive asset for others. This will lead you to achieve even greater success in life.

The Asset Mindset is a perspective from which everything is weighed or rated on an asset scale to see if it is a positive or negative asset to us in the pursuit of our life goals. If it is not positive, we do not want to waste our valuable asset of time on a negative. Ideally, when we live with *The Asset Mindset*, the only instance we will spend time on negative elements is when we work towards making them transform into something more positive. When a true understanding of *The Asset Mindset* philosophy is reached, you will have realized that no one influences your life more than you do, positively or negatively. You will put *The Asset Mindset* into action knowing you are your greatest asset while realizing that you are wiser and stronger due to your past experiences. While living with *The Asset Mindset,* we will be building positive habits and behaviors, knowing we are the creators of our future. When this level of awareness is achieved, you understand that you control your life's limitations and realize that your life's success can be limitless! Are you ready to live with *The Asset Mindset* philosophy and become limitless with your life's success?

The results you achieve while living with *The Asset Mindset* will undoubtedly change your life for the better. You will take ownership of your life, find more love in the world, and believe in yourself in a whole new way. The "How do I?" mentality will become your new normal when trying to achieve a goal. You will have the ability to control your thoughts more like a page master, allowing your mind to grow and expand in a positive manner. Living with *The Asset Mindset* will increase your motivation and help you show up more to achieve your life objectives, all while becoming more organized with your life and time.

You will begin to find and seek out opportunities and people who lift you up like a balloon, not drag you down like an anchor. Fear will be looked at differently realizing it is an opportunity for you to be courageous and achieve greatness. Remember, sometimes the greatest risks provide the greatest rewards. You will find yourself having more gratitude and purpose in life. Your daily behaviors and habits will become powerful tools for reaching success in your life. You will understand and believe that your life, and your accomplishments are in *your* control more than anyone or anything else's. All these things, and more, can be yours once you make the conscious decision to live your life with *The Asset Mindset*. You've already taken the first step. Now, you are ready to proceed!

For more visit: TheAssetMindset.com

Acknowledgements

I want to say THANK YOU to everyone who has ever done anything positive for me, mentored me, or guided me in the right direction in life, because I wouldn't be the man I am without you. *The Asset Mindset* was made possible by all of your contributions and amazing support. This book is a positive reflection on all of us.

Mom and Dad, thank you for loving me, teaching me about life, and raising me. I truly appreciate everything you did and taught me over the years.

To my wife Kimberly, you are a pillar of support and an amazing blessing! You are a true inspiration for me to keep pushing to better myself. You have given me my greatest gifts of love, our children Henry, Hazel, and Sophia. You have also supported the many hours, days, and months of writing to create *The Asset Mindset*. I am so grateful to you for allowing me to share some of your experiences with the world. You are such a beautiful strong woman. This book would not have been possible without you. Your insights, feedback, and the time you put into reading my many drafts was tremendously appreciated. Thank you so much for sharing your life and true self with me. I love you unconditionally.

To my children, you have taught me so much about genuine love, life, patience, and what it means to be a dad. All of you continue to show me on a regular basis what's truly precious in life. Each one of you can melt my heart with just your smile. Thank you so much for coming into this world to bless me with your presence and love. I will be forever grateful for all the gifts you have given me. I promise to always give you my love and support in this world and in the next. I love you with all my heart.

To my military brothers and sisters, and most of all my Special Forces brothers: thank you for all of the sacrifice, service, and support. To my former teammates and fellow Green Berets Brian, Chase, Leroy, Abel, Bob, Chaca, John, Alex, Josh, Bryan, Lou, CJ, and Mason, thank you for being in my life and allowing me to have the honor to serve with incredible men like you. You guys are the best this world has to offer! Thank you Dirty, Littleman, and Mr. Airman for accompanying me during segments of my military journey. I am truly humbled by all of your accomplishments and greatness. It was an honor for me to share some of our experiences together in *The Asset Mindset* .

Ryan, my fellow 18C and author, I can't thank you enough for all your service to our country, regiment, and for what you did to honor our mutual friend and fellow warrior Abe. I greatly appreciate you sharing your story with the world and allowing me to highlight some of it in my book.

Romy, thank you for allowing me to give my readers a glimpse into the extremely strong person you are. It was a privilege to spend the time I did with you while I was in 7th Special Forces Group. I can't say enough how impressive you are as a man, in and out of the military. You are an inspiration to us all!

Kid Rock, you are a great and extremely giving person, and a true friend who aided me in my transition back to civilian life. You brought me into your Kid Rock family, allowing me to experience life in a whole new way. I can't thank you enough for all you have done for me and all your positive contributions to our world. Thank you for letting me share a little about our experiences in my book.

I also want to thank those who shared words of encouragement and wisdom about writing with me. You definitely helped open doors, and mentored me as an author. I learned so much because of your kindness and willingness to share your time with me. Thank you Dave Ramsey, Chris Hogan, Ken Colman, and Melissa Wilson from Ramsey Solutions in Tennessee.

I want to especially thank those that put in lots of hours of their time polishing up my manuscript and giving me advice. *The Asset Mindset* would not be the quality product it is without you. Thank you so much Thomas Cirignano, Christopher Nochera, and Dr. Alice Atalanta.

Once again, *thank you all*. You are incredible *Asset Mindset Teammates!*

The Asset Mindset Recommended Reading List

- "The Power of Now," by Eckhart Tolle
- "Change Your Habits, Change Your Life," by Thomas C. Corley
- "Tip of The Spear," by, Ryan Hendrickson
- "The Proximity Principle," by Ken Coleman
- "The Constant Outsider: Memoirs of a South Boston Mechanic," and "67 Cents: Creation of a South Boston Killer," by Thomas M. Cirignano
- "Everyday Millionaire," by Chris Hogan
- "Stress Less Accomplish More," by Emily Fletcher
- "The Total Money Makeover," by Dave Ramsey
- "All Secure," by Tom Satterly
- "The 7 Habits of Highly Effective People," by Stephen R. Covey
- "Goals: How to Get the Most Out of Your Life," by Zig Ziglar
- "Looking Out for #1: How to get From Where You are Now to Where You Want to be in Life," and "Million Dollar Habits: 10 Simple Steps to Getting Everything You Want in Life," by Robert Ringer
- "Tuesdays with Morrie," by Mitch Albom
- "Rich Dad, Poor Dad," by Robert Kiyosaki
- "Boundaries," by Dr. Henry Cloud and Dr. John Townsend

The Asset Mindset Reader Notes

....

....

....

....

....

....

....

....

....

....

....

....

....

....

....

Notes

1. Ryan Hendrickson, "Tip of the Spear," (New York: Hachette, 2020), 57.

2. Tom Corley, "Change Your Habits, Change Your Life," (North Loop Books, 2016).

3. Robert Ringer, "Looking Out For #1," (New York: Sky Horse, 2013) 14.